Saint Sophia

Constantinople

*St. Sophia, Constantinople. Interior, looking west in 1849
after Fossati restoration (Fossati, 1852). [referenced as Fig 7]*

SAINT SOPHIA

AT
CONSTANTINOPLE

SINGULARITER
IN MUNDO

W. EUGENE KLEINBAUER

1999
WILLIAM L. BAUHAN, PUBLISHER
DUBLIN, NEW HAMPSHIRE

PUBLISHED FOR

THE ALLEN R. HITE ART INSTITUTE

UNIVERSITY OF LOUISVILLE

FREDERIC LINDLEY MORGAN CHAIR

OF ARCHITECTURAL DESIGN

Monograph No. 5

COPYRIGHT © 1999 BY THE ALLEN R. HITE ART INSTITUTE
UNIVERSITY OF LOUISVILLE
ALL RIGHTS RESERVED
LIBRARY OF CONGRESS CATALOGUING-IN-PUBLICATION DATA:

Kleinbauer, W. Eugene, 1937-
    Saint Sophia at Constantinople : singulater in mundo / W. Eugene
Kleinbauer.
    p.   cm. — (Monograph / Frederic Lindley Morgan Chair of
Architectural Design ; no. 5)
    "Published for the Allen R. Hite Art Institute, University of
Louisville"_T.p. verso .
    Includes bibliographical references.
    ISBN 0-87233-123-7 (alk. paper)
    1. Ayasofa Müzesi.   2. Architecture, Byzantine—Turkey—Istanbul.
3. Istanbul (Turkey)—Buildings, structures, etc.   I. Title.
II. Series: Monograph (Frederic Lindley Morgan Chair of
Architectural Design) ; no. 5.
NA5870.A9K64   1999
726'.5' 0949618—dc21   99-26569
                                                                          CIP

Foreword

EUGENE KLEINBAUER was the sixteenth holder of the
Frederic Lindley Morgan Chair of Architectural Design
at the University of Louisville. This study of Saint Sophia
grows out of his 1996 Morgan Lecture.

Trained at Berkeley and Princeton, and Professor of Fine
Arts and Near Eastern Languages at Indiana University for
more than twenty years, Dr Kleinbauer is one of the most
distinguished scholars of Early Christian and Byzantine art
and architecture. Author of *Early Christian and Byzantine
Architecture* (1992), and editor of *The Art of Byzantium and the
Medieval West* (1976), Professor Kleinbauer is writing a study
of the art and architecture of the Migrations with archae-
ologist and University of Louisville colleague, Stephanie
Maloney.

Frederic Lindley Morgan—Fred Morgan, who died in
1970, left his entire estate to the Allen R. Hite Institute for
the enrichment of its architectural offerings. That affable
Georgian Revival architect's gracious and inspired legacy
made Eugene Kleinbauer's seminar on Early Byzantine architecture and this subsequent book possible.

WILLIAM MORGAN
SERIES EDITOR

List of Illustrations

Introduction

To THOSE OF US who regularly work in the field, Eugene
Kleinbauer's bibliography *Early Christian and Byzantine Architecture* has become an indispensable tool. It is difficult to
imagine beginning a new project without consulting this
comprehensive and carefully executed resource. It is also
difficult to calculate the number of doctoral students who
have benefitted from the thorough historiographical introduction to that book when preparing for their exams. His
recognition and understanding of the most important writ-
ings of the twentieth century is reflected in his *Modern Per-
spectives in Western Art History* (1971, reprinted 1989) which,
for nearly three decades, has served as a fundamental text
in methods and theories classes.

Thrice honored as a distinguished teacher, Kleinbauer, in
his publications and papers, demonstrates not only his interest
in and knowledge of medieval art, architecture, and historiog-
raphy, but also his dedication to teaching. That dedication, and
the respect he has earned as a scholar and educator, has resulted in invitations to serve on external review teams for numerous colleges and universities and to participate in sympo-
sia on the teaching of Art History and its role in education.

Articles such as "Pre-Carolingian Concepts of Architectural Planning" (*The Medieval Mediterranean: Cross-Cultural
Contacts*, 1989) and "The Double-Shell Tetraconch Building
at Perge in Pamphylia and the Origin of Architectural Genus" (*Dumbarton Oaks Papers*, 41, 1987) are clear evidence of
Kleinbauer's understanding of architecture and of his care-

ful scholarship. In many ways the present monograph draws upon all of his talents and interests. Saint Sophia is surely one of the most-discussed buildings in the history of architecture. Contemporaries were awed by it and it astounds us today. Byzantine scholars almost inevitably refer to it at some point and many are compelled to write about it in detail, exploring it in terms of music, liturgy, design, structure, and so on. Virtually no author of a basic textbook or a book on Byzantine architecture would dream of leaving it out. The quantity of information about Saint Sophia is vast; it can be cumbersome for scholars and daunting for students. How, then, is this little book different from the rest?

Much of the emphasis of past scholarship has been on determining the sources for the design elements and the construction techniques employed by Anthemius and Isidorus. Instead of applauding the genius of its creators, scholars have seemed determined to show that Saint Sophia had to come from somewhere.

In this essay, Kleinbauer examines contemporary literature, as well as ancient sources in the light of his own comprehensive understanding of Byzantine architecture. He reexamines the validity of commonly-held assumptions, often tracing them back to their origins in his notes. His scholarship is careful and his ideas well-reasoned. As Kleinbauer himself states in his conclusions, his aim is "to demonstrate that its structure and design were *sui generis* rather than derivative" and, in a book so clearly written that students will find it invaluable and so thoroughly researched that scholars will be unable to ignore it, he achieves that goal.

STEPHANIE J. MALONEY

Preface

THIS STUDY is based on a Frederic Lindley Morgan Professorship Lecture sponsored by the Allen R. Hite Art Institute of the University of Louisville at the J. B. Speed Art Museum in March of 1996. Considerable material has been added, rearrangements have been made at certain points, and full documentation has been provided. I express my profound gratitude to Professor William Morgan, chair of the Morgan Professorship Committee, for allowing me to revise and expand the remarks made in that lecture in the form of this publication.

The aim of this publication is twofold. First, to try to envision the layout of the sixth-century church of St. Sophia of the emperor Justinian, to try to determine how the building was received by its contemporary audience as well as what the aims of its patron may have been. I undertake this task by assessing archeological remains, scientific studies of the surviving structural fabric, and sixth-century written sources on the church. My second aim is to evaluate what is known of the church building in terms of its concept and design. To what identifiable sources can we trace its individual salient features and the total compositional fabric of the monument? To what extent is Justinian's creation derivative and to what extent is it experimental? A considerable body of literature has appeared on St. Sophia in the last decade, much of it concerned with the issues that I address. References to these publications will be found in the notes.

Saint Sophia

The Nika Revolt

On January 13, 532, during the fifth year of the reign of the early Byzantine emperor Justinian the Great, Constantinople began to witness its most serious urban disturbance. This rioting was initiated by members of the two great factions of the Hippodrome, the Greens and the Blues. These factions were always a rowdy lot who frequently took to vandalism and the lighting of fires after a day at the horse races in the Hippodrome. On this occasion, having failed to obtain the release of some prisoners, and especially being quite discontent with the severe fiscal policy of Justinian and the extortions of his ministers, they joined forces and adopted as their slogan a password familiar in both the horse races and imperial acclamations, Nika ("Conquer"). What followed is known as the Nika revolt.[1] The insurrectionists made their way to the headquarters of the city prefect where they set fire to his building after having obtained the release of the prisoners. Fires spread through the city and in a few days destroyed various buildings in its central district, including the whole of the cathedral of St. Sophia, the forecourt of the nearby church of St. Irene, the hospice of Samson and all its patients, the Senate House, the Chalke (the bronze-roofed entrance to the imperial palace), and a number of other monuments.[2] Soon soldiers and even some senators joined forces with the Blues and Greens, and this mob proclaimed a man named Hypatius, a nephew of the emperor Anastasius (491-518), as the new emperor. For Justinian the situation had become desperate: his government had largely lost control of the city. Closeted in the palace with his trusted advisors, he was ready to flee by sea, but a rousing speech by his brainy wife Theodora is said to have been responsible for stiffening the resolve of the emperor and his advisors.[3] Whatever Theodora really said—we cannot be certain, Justinian decided to resist the rebellion and to bring loyal army units into play. Two of his trusted generals, Belisarius and Mundus, accompanied by loyal Goth troops, entered the Hippodrome where the rebels were assembled along with the usurper Hypatius, and a wholesale massacre ensued. 30,000 to 50,000 rebels are said to have been put to death by Justinian's forces.[4] Hypatius was arrested and executed, and the following day his remains tossed into the sea. The rebellious senators and patricians fled and their property was confiscated. A week after the riot had begun, the crisis had been resolved and the city was quiet.

ANTHEMIUS AND ISIDORE THE ELDER

Immediately after the suppression of this rebellion, Justinian set about rebuilding the edifices which had been destroyed or damaged by the conflagration. In this task his first priority seems to have been to rebuild the cathedral of St. Sophia. The emperor commissioned two men to undertake its rebuilding: they were Anthemius of Tralles (in Lydia) and the Elder Isidore of Miletus.[5] Contemporary writers refer to Anthemius and Isidore not as architects, though the term was common in the sixth century, but as *mechanikoi* or *mechanopoioi*. These terms denote a very small number of practitioners of the arts of design whether of buildings or of machines or other works, who were masters of the prevailing *mechanike theoria,* the "science of mechanics." This covers a far wider field than the modern science of mechanics and would have included just about all the subjects that a modern architect must master, not only the theory of geometry and physics, but also astronomy, which was more important in the ancient and late antique world than today.[6]

Anthemius was a mathematician and physicist who composed treatises such as *Concerning Remarkable Mechanical Devices, On Burning Mirrors* (an important document in the history of conic sections), and others on hydraulic subjects. In the words of the Byzantine writer Agathias (ca. 532–ca. 580), Anthemius was a scientist who applied "geometrical speculation to material objects and made models or imitations of the nature world."[7] The experiments of Anthemius included the production of an artificial earthquake, using steam power, and artificial thunder, as well as the creation of a powerful reflector.[8] To him we owe the first mention of the construction of an ellipse by means of a string stretched tight about the foci.[9] His colleague Isidore appears to have been a professor of geometry and mechanics who wrote a commentary on Heron of Alexandria's lost treatise *On Vaulting* of the late 1st century B.C. Isidore issued a revised edition of the works of Archimedes, was an authority on Euclid, and invented a compass for drawing parabolas.

Neither Anthemius nor Isidore is known to have had any building experience before their designing of the new St. Sophia,[10] and St. Sophia was not their only architectural work for Justinian. During a Persian siege in 540 the emperor consulted both of them about flood control at the eastern frontier city of Dara in Mesopotamia.[11] In the age of Justinian the range of expertise of *mechanopoioi* included major public works as well as church building. In short, two preeminent individuals possessing a high degree of technical knowledge and wide scientific interests rather than experienced architects or master builders were employed by Justinian to plan the new cathedral. The stage was set for the creation of a supremely innovative and daring monument. Work on the new St. Sophia may have been launched on February 23, 532, only some thirty-nine days after the end of the Nika riot.[12] The hymnographer Romanos the Melode (d. after 555) composed the poetic-homily "On Earthquakes and Fires" for the ceremony of the laying of the cornerstone of the new church, and this kontakion eulogizes Justinian for restoring the church and praises him as a new Solomon.[13] If the restoration of St. Sophia did in fact commence in late February of 532, Justinian may have intended to replace the old church with a new edifice before the outbreak of the Nika riot, although documentary sources do not confirm this.[14] If that was in fact his intention, we may inquire what would his motivation have been?

The Imperial Program

Justinian's St. Sophia needs to be understood in the light of his official imperial policies. His objectives are set forth by the sixth-century historian Procopius of Caesarea (in Palestine) at the beginning of his volume generally known as *De aedificiis* ("The Buildings"), written in all probability in the mid-550s, conceivably commissioned by Justinian, and either unfinished or at least unrevised.[15] This is the most detailed single record preserved of any ruler's building projects. Assuming power at a time of disorder along and

within the borders of the empire, Procopius writes in pan-
egyrical terms, Justinian expanded the extent of his domain,
creating an empire larger than had existed under his predecessors.[16] He reconquered the West from the Arian Goths,
and, at the same time, in the East secured the loyalty of his
provinces in the face of the Persian advances by placating
the Monophysite Christians of the region.[17] For Justinian
unity of the empire was absolutely fundamental. Accord-
ingly, remnants of paganism and all heresies such as
Arianism were banished, and one correct Orthodox faith
under one emperor was imposed. The emperor was the cre-
ator of internal harmony and external peace. Toward this
goal Justinian appointed a commission of ten lawyers to
undertake a most significant and sorely needed revision of
the legal system and an efficient means by which to admin-
istrate it: the result was issued as the Codex Justinianus. This
codification reflects the socioeconomic and ecclesiastical
problems of the times and contributed to the harmony of
the empire. But also these law codes term Justinian as the
Elect of God, king-priest, even archpriest, and reveal how
imperium and sacerdotium became more closely tied together than ever before.[18] This is not to say that Justinian
intended to usurp the authority of the Church. Politics and
religion—State and Church—became parallel branches of
one united Orthodox empire over which the emperor pre-
sided as God's vicegerent, his special representative on
earth.[19] But, most importantly, Procopius emphasizes that
Justinian undertook an imperial building program by con-
structing cities in reconquered territories, public works and
ecclesiastical monuments in Constantinople and the most
diverse parts of the empire, and above all fortifications all
along the outer borders of his domain.[20] He terms him
"builder of the world."[21]

Although military architecture is clearly emphasized by Procopius's "The Buildings," church construction or restoration assumed enormous importance in Justinian's building program.[22] Procopius claims that Justinian built or restored thirty-three churches at Constantinople and its suburbs alone, and he names or implies the presence of Justinianic church constructions at over seventy different sites as far away the remote town of Septum (modern Ceuta) in Vandal Africa, not far from the Strait of Gibraltar.[23] But he does not offer a comprehensive or necessarily reliable record of the emperor's architectural undertakings. Other sources provide documentation of other Justinianic projects overlooked by or unknown to Procopius. For example, the Syriac historian John of Ephesus (ca. 507-586 or 588), who had been successful in tracking down heathens in Constantinople, asserts that Justinian built ninety-six churches and twelve monasteries in the towns and countryside of the provinces of Asia, Phrygia, Lydia, and Caria in western Asia Minor where pagan cults still survived.[24] Fifty-five of the ninety-six churches were paid for by the imperial treasury. John was sent in 542 by Justinian as a missionary to these provinces to terminate the heathen practices of the pagans (termed "Hellenes") and to convert them to the true Orthodox faith. John claims that he converted 70,000 persons, with the emperor paying for the baptismal vestments of the converts and giving each of them a small sum of money. The conversion of pagans was one of the aims of Justinian's program of building churches.[25]

The key monument in Justinian's ecclesiastical architectural program was the rebuilding of St. Sophia in his capital city. It is this church with which Procopius begins *De aedificiis*, and far more space is devoted to it than any other building project, ecclesiastical or secular, in any part of the empire. To be sure, Constantinople had to have a cathedral and other churches in which the emperor and his subjects as well as the patriarch who was the chief hierarch of the Eastern Church could pray and attend services. But for Justinian simply restoring St. Sophia to its former design would not suffice. The cathedral had to reflect fully grand imperial munificence in general and the imperial ideology of Justinian himself. It had to represent a symbol of Justinian's own imperial authority, to glorify the emperor as the representative on earth of the divine power in heaven. And as an architectural enterprise it had to overwhelm the martyr shrines elsewhere in the capital and in all other cities, including Rome. Justinian must have viewed the opportunity of rebuilding the cathedral, whether either before or immediately after the Nika Revolt, to further imperial power over the church—all in the name of establishing harmony and unity in his domain.

The Byzantine poet Paul the Silentiary reciting a long encomiun in honor of St. Sophia soon after its second consecration on December 24, 562, speaks of the significance of the church:

> Indeed, our emperor, who has gathered all manner of wealth from the whole earth, from barbarians and Ausonians (i.e., his own subjects) alike, did not deem a stone adornment sufficient for this divine, immortal temple in which Rome has placed all its proud joys of hope.[26]

Of the day of the reconsecration of the church the poet declares that "God and emperor are celebrated together."[27]

Justinian's St. Sophia was built in five years and ten months, seemingly an incredibly short period of time for a building of its scale and complexity. It took more than eighty years to complete Constantine's Old St. Peter's in Rome, thirty-two years to build the Gothic cathedral of Chartres beginning in 1194, Salisbury Cathedral more than forty years. Had Justinian been content simply to restore the ruined St. Sophia to its previous design, the church could perhaps have been completed in about two years.[28] But, as I have suggested, he wanted something different, radically different. The main driving force behind the redesigning of St. Sophia, the emperor had the financial resources for the project and assembled a huge work force. According to the Narratio concerning the building of St. Sophia, an anonymous, semilegendary source of the ninth century, there were 100 master masons, each of whom had a gang of 100 men under him, hence 10,000 in all.[29] Whatever its actual size, the teams of workmen were well organized, and the logistics impeccable. Given the short period of time in which the church was completed, it seems likely that the engineer-architects, masons, carvers, mosaicists, and other artisans worked together rather than independently. Anthemius and Isidore had to draw up an architectural brief and obtain the emperor's approval. The brief may well have included plans, elevations, and perspectival drawings or projections, but we may question whether there was systematic advance planning of all details of the entire enterprise.[30] Procopius specifically reports that Anthemius prepared "in advance designs (*indalmata*) of the future construction."[31] Sufficient materials had to be procured, and they are alleged to have come from as far away as Rome.[32] The remains of the old church had to be razed and the rubble cleared away. Part of the site of the church had to expropriated, for it was allegedly occupied by a number of private dwellings.[33] Hence the site of the new church was programmed to exceed that of the Theodosian church. Although unrecorded, the emperor imposed some sort of system of administrative regu-

lations, no doubt more elaborate than those he had set up
for the construction in the year 531 of the Nea (New Church)
in honor of the Virgin at Jerusalem.[34] Once actual construction of the new St. Sophia commenced, it proceeded quickly,
at least until the great arches below the central dome were
under construction, when unforeseen major structural problems developed, as recounted by Procopius, and which will
be mentioned below. As the church went up, changes and
modifications were made and some new forms were invented
which altered the original building program. Such a pro-
cess of change is known to have characterized the construction of Gothic cathedrals in France centuries later.

ST. SOPHIA BEFORE JUSTINIAN

The new St. Sophia was inaugurated on December 27, 537
by the patriarch Menas.[35] It replaced the earlier cathedral
at the site which had been first built under the emperor
Constantius II (337-61) and dedicated in 360.[36] Preceded by a
forecourt or atrium, the church of Constantius II was a
wooden-roofed basilica with a nave flanked by two or perhaps four side aisles, each carrying a gallery story, perhaps
much like the Constantinian basilica of the Holy Sepulcher at Jerusalem.[37] Later Byzantine sources mention marble
columns in the fourth-century St. Sophia.[38] A baptistery
known as "Olympas" stood inside or probably adjacent to
the church,[39] and an episcopal palace of at least two stories
was attached to its south side.[40] The first St. Sophia was
known as the Great Church (*he megale ekklesia*)—the name
St. Sophia, referring to Christ as the Wisdom (*Sophia*) of
God is first attested only ca. 430.[41] The cathedral of
Constantius burned in the year 404 but there is no report

on how extensive the damage was. Since the church was func-
tioning again by 406, it must have been limited.[41A] The
church was repaired or rebuilt by the emperor Theodosius
II (408-450) and rededicated in 415. Whether the original
fourth-century planning was changed under Theodosius II
remains undocumented. Remnants of the fourth- and the
early fifth-century churches are visible today in front of
the entrance of the present church and in its courtyard. They
consist of the flight of six steps leading up to the stylobate
of a monumental portico and, about 4 m. eastward, the
stretch of an early wall. A sufficient number of architectural blocks belonging to the portico were excavated by
Alfons Maria Schneider in 1935, who demonstrated that the
center of the entrance portico projected from the monumental colonnade and featured a pedimental porch with an
arcuated lintel. As Schneider showed, the style of the sculp-
tural ornament of these blocks discloses that they were
carved in the time of Theodosius II. The stretch of the
early wall to the east of this portico is most probably the
eastern wall of the atrium rather than the church itself.[42] It
is constructed of alternate bands of brickwork and of mortared rubble work, faced with courses of small, very roughly
square stone (currently capped by several courses of modern masonry). The pre-Justinianic church was smaller than
its sixth-century replacement, seems to have been aligned
at an angle of about a couple of degrees further toward the
south, and consisted of elements that were standard features of Constantinopolitan church planning in the early
Byzantine period: an atrium, perhaps a narthex, and an aisled
basilica with galleries.[43] These basic features provide important roots of the planning of Justinian's St. Sophia.

JUSTINIAN'S FIRST CHURCH

As for St. Sophia, Divine Wisdom, the human mind
can neither tell it nor make description of it.[44]

Justinian's replacement of the old St. Sophia is essentially what stands today (Fig. 1). Because it is so complex an architectural enterprise, it is difficult to analyze, to visualize comprehensively, and to represent graphically.[45] It may be described as an expanded domed basilica[46], that is, a rectangular shaped building covered by a central dome between two half-domes and integrating longitudinal and centralized planning, 69.7 by 74.6 m. internally, excluding the two

Fig. 1 St. Sophia, Constantinople. West facade (Fine ArtsPhoto Archives, Indiana University)

narthexes and the large colonnaded atrium which measured
47.7 by 32.3 m. , providing a total length of approximately
134.72 m. (Fig. 2).[47] As was customary in the early church
planning of Constantinople, numerous entrances in the
outer narthex as well as each of the other three perimeter
walls gave access to the interior; although the exact number
is unknown, there were up to forty doors in Byzantine
times.[48] Access to the galleries of St. Sophia was obtained
by exterior staircase towers; such towers with ramps are a
traditional feature of Constantinopolitan church planning,
documented as early as about the middle of the fifth century. Preceding the nave of St. Sophia on the west are two
narthexes, a feature unknown in the other pre-Iconoclastic
church buildings of the city.[49] The outer narthex was in
effect the eastern wing of the atrium and was completely
enclosed and vaulted over, while the inner narthex could be
entered through five doors from it and gave access to the
nave of the church by nine doors. Marble plaques once
sheathed the west facade and possibly the entire exterior of
the church.[50] Although the exterior of the building has been
significantly altered since the sixth century, a contemporary viewed the whole building "as fittingly proportioned"
in breadth and length, combining "its mass with the harmony of its proportions."[51]

The center of the nave is a square bay 30.975 m. on a
side marked off by four prodigious piers which rise 23.14
m. and are spanned by four thick semicircular arches bound
together by pendentives (Fig. 3). The four pendentives rise
to a height of 41.5 m. and are of an unprecedented scale.
From the crown of each of the main piers and between
the four great arches the pendentives fan out on the interior and rise to a roughly circular projecting cornice constructed of flat marble blocks upon which the base of the

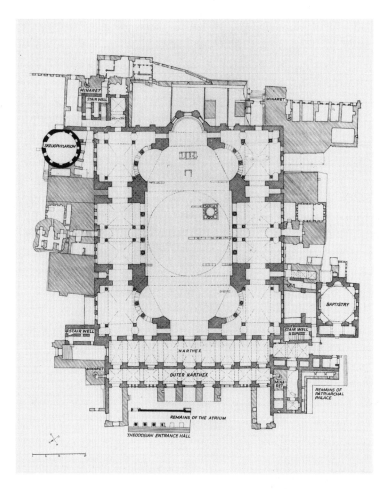

Fig 2. St. Sophia, Constantinople. Ground plan, by R. L. Van Nice (Fine Arts Photo Archives, Indiana University)

*Fig 3. St. Sophia, Constantinople. Interior to east, c.1902
(Messbildanstalt, Berlin)*

dome and a catwalk for lamplighters and maintenance persons rest.[52] Measuring approximately 31 m. in diameter,[53] the dome soars above the marble pavement to a height of 55.6 m. Built entirely of brick and mortar, it rises 15.0 m. from the level of the upper cornice and is not a true hemisphere of 180 degrees but subtends an angle of 163 degrees, so that its center of curvature is appreciably below the level of the cornice.[54] It consists of forty concave webs separated by forty evenly spaced ribs, with forty arched windows between the ribs at its base.[55] This corona of windows provides an important source of natural lighting to which I will return.

The domed center space is flanked by two large hemicycles covered by half-domes to the east and west (Fig. 4). The diameter of these half-domes about equals that of the central dome. The base of each half-dome is fenestrated with a ring of five windows, providing another source of natural illumination. The creative genius of the design of Anthemius and the Isidore the Elder is evident in the open expansion of the tall central block of domed space by the pair of spacious hemicycles covered by half-domes, placed along the major east-west axis of the monument in a balanced composition uninterrupted by walls, piers, or columns (Fig. 5). These core spaces are separated from one aisle to the north and another to the south by superposed colonnades, with galleries over the side aisles and inner narthex, creating a U-shape which reinforces the centralizing tendency of this "expanded domed basilica"—another established feature of local church planning. Curved columnar exedrae billow out in both stories at the diagonals of the hemicycles toward the corners of the aisles and galleries, and each of the exedrae is covered by a semidome again pierced by a ring of windows (Fig. 6). The placement of the piers of these exedrae transform the nave of the edifice into an oval configuration, the first time in the history of the basilican church building that such planning had occurred. This central oval vessel of enclosed space is further expanded by barrel-vaulted spaces which terminate along the building's longitudinal axis at the east and west ends of its nave. An almost semicircular window divided into three areas by two intermediate columns opens up the full width of the barrel vault at the west end of the nave, the largest surviving window in the edifice (Fig. 7). By contrast, the semicircular wall of the apse at the east end of the nave is pierced by two rows of three round-arched windows, each roughly corresponding to the two stories of the elevation of the church, while another ring of five smaller arched windows sits near the base of the semidome of the apse (Fig. 8).

2 6   W. EUGENE KLEINBAUER

The lateral thrusts of the dome and two half-domes, including their dead loads, are concentrated at only twelve points—the main and secondary piers and buttresses (Fig. 2). For the enclosure of such a vast space this is an ingenious deployment of piers and buttresses which occupy only six to eight per cent of the floor area of the church—about 18,000 square meters, roughly the equivalent of three and a half football fields.[56]

The original dome, like the second dome, of the church was supported by four pendentives, and these are described by Procopius immediately after discussing the four great arches connecting the main piers:

> And since the arches are joined together on a square plan, the intervening construction assumes the form of four triangles (i.e., the pendentives). The bottom end of each triangle, being pressed together by the conjunction of the arches, causes the lower angle to be acute, but as it rises it becomes wider by the intervening space and terminates in the arc of a circle, which it supports, and forms the remaining (two) angles at that level.[57]

Such length in describing a single constructional device of the church would seem to imply an unusual feature. In any event, Procopius's account of the pendentives is followed by a far more succinct description of the central dome, "suspended from heaven by that golden chain," quoting Homer's vision of Zeus suspending the whole earth from Mount Olympus in the *Iliad*.[58] The nave of St. Sophia is audaciously spacious, about three times wider than of any Gothic cathedral in transalpine Europe, and the central dome attains the height of a fifteen-story building, significantly higher than the tallest Gothic vaults. (At Beauvais Cathedral in France the early thirteenth-century vaults of the choir reached 46 m., the highest vaults of any

Fig 4. St. Sophia, Constantinople. Fish eye view of vaulting (Courtesy Rizzoli)

known Gothic building, but in 1284 they collapsed.) The interior of no other building of the Middle Ages any-where in Europe or the Middle East attained the height of St. Sophia. Nor earlier had the Romans or Byzantines themselves constructed such a lofty space. The spectacular achievement of Justinian's church did not escape the attention of contemporaries, who were amazed by it. For Procopius, the church

> soars to a height to match the sky, and as if surging up from amongst the other buildings it stands on high and looks down upon the remainder of the city, adorning it, because it is a part of it, but glorifying in its own beauty, because, though a part of the city and dominating it, it at the same time towers above it to such a height that the whole city is viewed from there as from a watch tower.[59]

Boldly and subtly integrated with the sweeping verticality of the interior is the horizontality created by the arcades of the ground floor and galleries embracing the nave and the gallery and upper cornices. For the first time in the history of the basilican church building the apse at the end of the nave ceases to be the focal point of the design. Now the entire space of the nave invites the eye of the spectator to take in the totality of its ever rising undulating surfaces and glazed openings and to behold the hovering central dome and two adjacent half-domes. And yet, as Procopius correctly related already in his day, all of the elements of the upper reaches of the church

> do not allow the spectators to rest their gaze upon any one of them for a length of time, but each detail readily draws and attracts the eye to itself. Thus the vision constantly shifts round, and the beholders are quite unable to select any particular elements which they might admire more than the others.[60]

Justinian's nave exhibits a dynamic soaring fluidity generated by the openness and unprecedented system of curves and counter-curves of the vaults, arches, cornices, and windows.

Its hugeness contrasts markedly with the smaller scale of

the enveloping aisles and galleries which do not echo the openness of the nave, as in earlier Byzantine basilican churches. Rather, these peripheral corridors are compartmentalized into bays by arches spanning their widths and the domical vaults and barrel vaults entirely covering them in both stories. In contrast to earlier church building, these bays are interlocked rather than additive units placed side by side.

Another significant major feature of the design of the church interior is the lack of correspondence in the colonnades of the ground floor and gallery (Figs. 5-6). The diameter and height of the columns and the intercolumniations between the main piers and in the curved exedrae differ in the two stories. Between the main piers to the north and south four columns of verde antico (10.36 m. in height) supporting five arches stand on the pavement, and six supporting seven arches in the second story, while in the exedrae two (probably monolithic) porphyry columns (ranging from 7.3 m. to 7.62 m. in height) supporting three arches stand below and four verde antico supporting arches above.[61] This is the first time in the history of early Byzantine architecture that the disposition of columns at gallery level is not lined up with those on the ground floor; and such a deployment is virtually non-existent in pre-Byzantine buildings.[62] Originally in the mid-fifth century basilica of St. John Studius, and later in Justinian's church of SS. Sergius and Bacchus in Constantinople (Fig. 11), an exact vertical alignment obtains in both stories.[63] And in these two churches the ground-floor colonnades are crowned by an entablature, whereas in St. Sophia they are arcuated. The arrangement of the colonnades in St. Sophia is in this respect completely novel and unclassical, as was recognized already by Paul the Silentiary referring to the arrangement in the curved exedrae: "one may wonder at the resolve of the man who

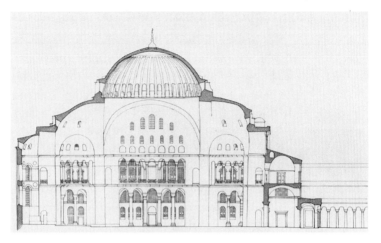

Fig 5. St. Sophia, Constantinople. Longitudinal section, by R. L. Van Nice (Fine Arts Photo Archives, Indiana University)

upon two columns has bravely set thrice two, and has not hesitated to fix their bases over empty air."[64] Possibly the original building program called for a far greater harmony in the superposed sets of colonnades, as the balanced designs of the interiors of the apse and the west end of the church suggest (Fig. 7). Yet the four large columns between the great piers rest on low bases, while the porphyry shafts contrastingly rise from white pedestals, surely the initial disposition of these elements. After the ground-floor colonnades had been constructed Anthemius and Isidore the Elder may have been decided to make a radical change because columns of the size of the verde antico and porphyry ones on the ground floor could not be obtained for the second story, necessitating the use of smaller columns in the second story.[65] The use of smaller columns at gallery level also resulted in reduced intercolumniations and a reduction of the cross section of the four main piers. Whatever the cause, these changes produce a greater openness and weightlessness in the gallery colonnades, and these distinctive aspects of the design correspond to the dematerialization of the structure which gradually increases from the ground floor to the half-domes and central dome sailing overhead (Fig. 3).

THE JUSTINIANIC REBUILDING OF ST. SOPHIA

Along with the eastern main arch and the eastern half-dome, the original dome of Anthemius and Isidore the Elder collapsed in May, 558, after a series of earthquakes in the preceding four years.[66] Its design is in dispute. It surely featured a slightly elliptical shape, as the eyewitness Agathias indicates, but this shape was caused by the outward tilting of the north and south piers and arches during construction and had not been originally intended (Fig. 8).[67] The short-lived central covering of Anthemius and Isidore the Elder was either a pendentive dome or a dome on pendentives, probably with a fenestrated drum and catwalk, as in the present dome.[68] Whatever its exact configuration, the original dome constituted the principal feature of the first St. Sophia, and it struck the sixth-century beholder with more astonishing amazement than did its replacement.[69]

The original dome was rebuilt by the mechanipoios Isidore of Miletus the Younger, a nephew of the Elder Isidore of Miletus (who had died).[70] Before he had been put in charge of the replacement of the dome in 558 Isidore the Younger had distinguished himself in the rebuilding of city ramparts in the provinces. Procopius reports that the emperor Justinian had him rebuild the city walls of Chalcis in northern Syria in 550, and this is confirmed by two preserved inscriptions.[71] While Isidore the Younger was still a

*Fig 6. St. Sophia, Constantinople. Interior, north-west exedra
(Fine Arts Photo Archives, Indiana University)*

young man he was an associate of the mechanipoios John, a
native of Constantinople, in the fortifying of the strong-
hold city of Zenobia on the Euphrates River in Syria.[72]
Isidore the Younger's replacement of the dome of St. Sophia

Fig 7. St. Sophia, Constantinople. Interior, looking west in 1849 after Fossati restoration (Fossati, 1852)

took more than two-thirds the time it initially took to construct the entire church in the 530s. Completion occurred
by the time the cathedral was reconsecrated on December
24, 562, while Justinian still occupied the throne. Remark-

ably, Isidore the Younger's dome has survived for over 1400 years to the present day, although rebuilt in part. One third of the dome (thirteen ribs) and the western arch collapsed after an earthquake in 989 and were rebuilt by the celebrated Armenian architect Trdat, while the east semidome, the great east arch, and another one third of the dome (another thirteen ribs) collapsed in 1346 after a series of earthquakes in 1343 and 1344—these elements were rebuilt by 1354 under the supervision of Phakeolatos and the architects the grand stratopedarches ("military commander") Astras and the Latin subject John Peralta.[73] The tenth- and fourteenth-century rebuildings of the dome were closely based on the sixth-century design of Isidore the Younger, even if the quality of workmanship suffered in comparison. The design of his dome is the one that survives today.

Aside from the first dome of the church, no dome of such daring scale and design had ever been constructed at Constantinople or elsewhere in the early Byzantine world. Nor did it have any successors in Byzantium. For some eight hundred years St. Sophia remained the largest vaulted structure in the world, and it has today the third largest masonry dome.

Other major changes in the design of the original church of 532 to 537 include the rebuilding of the north and south tympanums in their present form, probably sometime after an earthquake of 869 damaged the structure.[74] At least after Isidore the Younger rebuilt the dome the north and south tympanums featured larger fenestrated areas than today, admitting a greater amount of light to the interior. Massive exterior buttresses were constructed on the north and east sides of the building in 1317.[75] The four flying buttresses now leaning against the upper narthex wall have often been thought to represent the work of the Crusaders in the thirteenth century, but Mainstone's recent reassessment of these

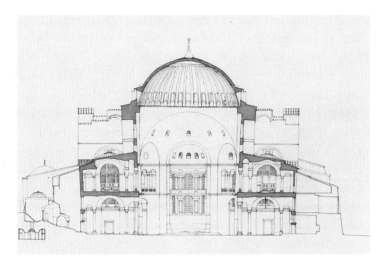

Fig 8. St. Sophia, Constantinople. Transverse section, by R. L. Van Nice (Fine Arts Photo Archives, Indiana University)

devices suggests that it is more likely they were added either after 869 or in 989; if true, they are the earliest recorded flying buttresses in the history of architecture (Fig. 1).[76] The minarets at the four corners of the building were added by the Ottoman Turks after they had conquered Constantinople and converted St. Sophia into a mosque (Ayasofya Camii) in 1453.[77] In the following century the great Ottoman architect Sinan added the pair of minarets at the western corners.[78] The Ottomans also erected the various sultans' mausolea on the north, south, and west sides of their mosque.[79] The church itself has been repaired several times, the first and most important in 1573, and again in 1847-49 by the Swiss architect Gaspare Fossati, assisted by his brother Giuseppe.[80] Under the Fossatis eight colossal circular green levhas or placards (8 m. in diameter) bearing golden letters of Holy Names were hung from the faces of the piers at gallery level (Fig. 7).[81] The present Koranic inscription in the dome replaced an earlier inscription, which, in turn, replaced a Pantokrator figure of the fourteenth century.[82] In 1739 an library was erected by the sultan Mahmut I in the south aisle, and two centuries later a loge for sultan Abdül Mecit was constructed to the north of the apse.[83] Today all the furnishings and lamps in the monument today are Ottoman installations. In 1934 Ayasofya Camii was secularized and the next year became a public state museum, its function to the present day. Beginning in that year the Byzantine Institute of America began to bring to light a number of iconic Christian mosaics in the new museum, all postdating the Iconoclastic Controversy and located throughout the main body of the building and now visible.[84] Coming down to us from the age of Justinian, however, are a number of aniconic, decorative mosaics.[85]

Many of the original subsidiary structures and other surrounding features of the church of Justinian can be visualized in part. Partially preserved in part until the nineteenth century, the atrium of Justinian's church has today disappeared. Retrieved by Schneider's excavations of 1935, it was rectangular, wider than it was long (47.7 by 32.3 m.) and colonnaded on three sides, with an alternating support system of piers and columns on the north, south and west sides. The outer narthex of the church made up its fourth side. Paul the Silentiary reports that the center of the atrium at the west end of the church was occupied up by a large fountain (phiale) made of Carian marble and emitting streams of water.[86] The poet also mentions that "outside the divine church you may see everywhere, along its flanks and boundaries, many open courts" so that the church "may appear bathed all round by the bright light of day."[87] Earlier churches in Constantinople also featured enveloping courtyards.[88] The urban space of the city was quite crowded in the day of Justinian. According to the eyewitness testimony of Agathias "the fact is that every quarter of the city is so heavily built up that wide open spaces entirely free of obstructions are an extremely rare sight."[89] The courtyards of Justinian's cathedral enhanced and accentuated its prominence as a religious and urban symbol on the former acropolis of Byzantium. By 1672 when Guillaume-Joseph Grelot visited Constantinople the courtyards of St. Sophia had been demolished and replaced by Turkish garden courtyards on its west, south, and north sides.[90] Grelot illustrates two of the Turkish courtyards in his engravings which may convey an approximate impression of their Byzantine predecessors (Fig. 9).[91]

A large Byzantine baptistery ("the Great Baptistery") of unknown configuration was situated somewhere on the north side of the church; all trace of it has disappeared.[92] Built under Justinian, a smaller baptistery (the "Little Baptistery"), octagonal in plan, still stands just to the south west of the church, near its modern entrance (Fig. 2).[93] A remnant of the patriarchal palace is preserved at the south end of the west gallery,[94] while near the southwest porch stands the horologion or clock building, possibly of Justinianic date, though this is unsubstantiated.[95] The pre-Justinianic skeuophylakion sits close to the northeast corner of the building.[96] Three exterior stair ramps giving access to the galleries are preserved and a fourth ramp may have existed at the south east.[97]

From the beginning St. Sophia belonged to a sacred space that included the church of St. Eirene, situated about 110 m. to its north. St. Eirene may have been constructed on the site of a pre-Constantinian Christian church, for it was referred to as the Old Church (he palaia ecclesia). The church historian Socrates reports that the emperor Constantine the

Fig 9. St. Sophia, Constantinople. Exterior, from the northwest in 1680 (Grelot)

Great enlarged and adorned this old church, which together with St. Sophia was enclosed by a common wall and was served by the same body of clergy as St. Sophia.[97a] And St. Eirene served as the main church of the city while St. Sophia

was being repaired after 404, and it might have been the site
of the Council of Constantinople in 381. It was severely
damaged or destroyed during the Nike riot of 532. This common clergy also served a third church in this sacred complex, that of the Theotokos of Chalkoprateia, erected under the emperor Theodosius II (408-50), possibly by his sis-
ter Pulcheria (399-453), about 100 m. west of St. Sophia in
the quarter of the coppersmiths.[97b] This church served as
the patriarchal church while St. Sophia and St. Eirene were
being redesigned and rebuilt by Justinian beginning in 532.[97c]

INTERIOR DECORATION

Colored marbles in the form of columns and wall facings
adorn the nave, aisles, galleries, and narthex of the first
church of Justinian. The marble shafts of the columns are
complexly arranged in terms of size, proportion, and color:
de novo green columns of Thessalian marble between the
four main piers on the ground floor and reused porphyry
columns on the ground floor of the curved exedrae, while
green carries all the way through in the galleries (Fig. 6).[98]
The column shafts carry capitals of white marble. The sophisticated alternation of groups of columns of differently
colored marbles on the ground floor is paralleled in the nave
and tribelon of the church of St. Demetrius at Thessaloniki.
Although the dating of the first church of St. Demetrius is
controversial, recent examination of its fabric indicates that
it was first laid out in its present form around the beginning
of the reign of Justinian.[99]

The marbles of St. Sophia capture the attention of the
contemporary beholder as they did of the sixth-century

Byzantine audience, as we know from Procopius and Paul
the Silentiary. In the words of Procopius:

> Who could recount the beauty of the columns and the
> marbles with which the church is adorned? One might imag-
> ine that one has chanced upon a meadow in full bloom. For
> one would surely marvel at the purple hue of some, the
> green of others, at those on which the crimson blooms, at
> those that flash with white, at those, too, which Nature, like
> a painter, has varied with the most contrasting colors.[100]

Paul the Silentiary also observes that the marble revetments
of St. Sophia resemble the art of painting.[101] The poet mentions twelve varieties of "marble meadows gathered upon
the mighty walls and spreading pavement of the lofty
church."[102] All these varieties can still be seen in the church
despite major losses.[103] There were black stone from the
Bosporus region, with white streaks; green marble from
Carystus in Greece; polychrome stone from Phrygia; porphyry flecked with silver from Egypt; an emerald green
marble from Sparta; an Isaurian marble with red and white
veins; yellow stone from Libya, onyx, and other rare marbles.
The floor was paved with local Proconnesian marble (much
of which survives),[104] interrupted by bands of green marble
running across from north to south, while all wall surfaces
were sheathed in thin marble plaques up to the springings
of the impost of the vaults and arches. In the nave the piers
and walls are generally faced with tall slabs of different
colors arranged in three registers.[105] From a single block the
slabs were sliced in two and fitted together so that their natural veining forms symmetrical patterns along a central axis.
These facings measure only about 20 to 30 millimeters in
thickness. Simple white fillet moldings of marble frame the
double slabs, tall single slabs, and all horizontal bands. Although the interior walls of Christian buildings were faced

with marbles as early as the fourth century, the system of revetment in St. Sophia, with narrow marble plaques of one color (as opposed to architectural pilaster strips in marble) framing larger panels of different colors, possibly originates in this church. These polychromatic facings not only conceal the stones and bricks of the piers and walls but also dematerialize them, creating a sense of diaphanous insubstantiality and of actual fluidity. The same is true of the shimmering gold mosaics that already in the 530s completely sheathed the central dome, half-domes, and vaults throughout the fabric.[106] The center of the dome of Isidore the Younger was ornamented with a huge mosaic cross within a circle, "so that the Savior of the whole world may for ever protect the church."[107]

The spandrels and soffits of the colonnades on the ground floor are faced with white marble that is deeply undercut to form a system of lacelike foliate ornamentation with continuous tendrils coiling their way freely over the surface, seemingly suspended in front of a dark ground. At the level of the galleries *opus sectile* work features luxuriant forms resembling those carved on the ground-floor spandrels. This decoration is unabashedly unclassical.

Likewise the capitals. A variety of capital types is found in the church, all of them executed in white marble.[108] On both floors the green marble shafts of the main colonnades and the porphyry shafts in the four exedrae carry "bowl" capitals capped by small Ionic volutes, the sharply and deeply undercut surfaces of which are treated like the spandrels above (Fig. 10). These capitals display acanthus and palm leaves. The unclear ancestry of the bowl capital should not obscure the inventiveness of its type. The type is quite distinct from that of the "fold capitals" in the lower story of the roughly contemporary Justinianic church of SS. Sergius

Fig 10. St. Sophia, Constantinople. Bowl capital in south gallery (Photo: Kleinbauer)

and Bacchus at Constantinople (Fig. 11). At least some of the carved capitals of St. Sophia were gilded,[109] and bosses on the capitals bear monograms, mostly of Justinian, or emperor (*Basileus*), but also, though rarely, of Theodora, or empress (*Augusta*). No two of the bowl capitals or monograms are exactly identical, reflecting a not insignificant degree of freedom exercised by their carvers. By contrast, throughout the aisles and galleries of the church behind the main order carved Ionic impost capitals and carved impost blocks occur, though they too are of white marble.

In daylight the interior of the church was flooded by rays

of light streaming in through countless windows of different sizes. One wonders whether Justinian's church was more extensively fenestrated that any previous church building in the Greek East or Latin West. As the worshiper entered the central nave of the church from the inner narthex on a sunny morning the first impression received was a matrix of rays of light pouring in through the numerous windows in the eastern walls of the building and flooding the interior. Paul the Silentiary mentions that through the forty-arched windows of the second dome "the rays of fair-haired Dawn are channeled."[110] For Procopius the church "abounds exceedingly in gleaming sunlight." He recounts that the reflection of the sunlight from the marbles made one think that the church was "not illuminated by the sun from the outside, but that the radiance is generated within, so great an abundance of light bathes this shrine all around." [111] But the tonality of the sixth-century light was possibly more subdued than at present owing, I suspect, to lost colored glass window panes, such as have been found in the Justinianic church of San Vitale at Ravenna, the "Lower City Church" at Amorium, and in post-Iconoclastic Byzantine churches in Constantinople.[112]

The sixth-century Greek kontakion composed for the inauguration of the church offers an interpretation of this interior light:

> This sacred church of Christ evidently outstrips in glory even the firmament above, for it does not offer a lamp of merely sensible light, but the shine of it bears aloft the divine illumination of the Sun of Truth and it is splendidly illumined throughout by day and by night by the rays of the Word of the Spirit, through which the eyes of the mind are enlightened by him (who said) 'Let there be light!', God. [113]

The multitude of windows piercing the walls of St. Sophia

admits light, making the church a repository of light, and
light stands for wisdom (*sophia*) and the salvation which it
brings. This reference to light should be related to the dedication of the church to Christ, the Word of God, Light of
the World, Savior of Mankind, the Light and Resurrection
of All—*hagia Sophia.*[114]

A blaze of light inundated the interior at night as well,
according to the testimony of the poet Paul: a "nocturnal
sun filled the majestic temple with light."[115] From the dome
were suspended "long twisted chains of beaten brass, linked
in alternating curves by many hooks," forming a "united
circling choir" before they reached the pavement and to
which were attached silver discs holding fine-wrought glass
vessels, floating in "a circle above the heads of men." "For
in the circle you will see, close to the discs, the symbol of a
lofty cross with many eyes upon it." And in a second smaller
inner circle he recounts that there is a second crown bearing lamps around its rim, and in the "very center another
noble disc rises shining in the air, so that darkness is made
to flee." He goes on to describe other lamps suspended in
the aisles and around the colonnades and the walls, and these
too were set in silver vessels, some suspended in mid-air
and at different heights and some standing on the pavement.
Yet additional lamps formed a circle of light around the
dome cornice, and there were lights on the chancel screen.
As a result of this myriad of lamps, "... the bright night smiles
like the day and appears herself to be rosy-ankled."[116]

LITURGICAL FURNISHINGS

The sanctuary of the first church of Justinian was provided
with liturgical furnishings many of which were presum-

ably destroyed when the central dome collapsed in 558. Aside from the report of Procopius that these furnishings were embellished with 40,000 pounds of silver, we have no information about the initial liturgical layout and its fittings.[117] After the collapse of the dome and before the second inauguration of the church in 562 these furnishings were rebuilt and perhaps in part redesigned, and they are described in detail by Paul the Silentiary who devotes about one-third of his descriptive poem to them.[118]

In the apse was installed a *synthronon* of seven semicircular steps, the topmost one of which was occupied by a clergy seats flanking the patriarchal throne in the center, all sheathed in silver. Perhaps surviving the dome's collapse in 558, it is widely assumed that the synthronon bore resemblance in layout to that which is still extant in the apse of the nearby Justinianic church of St. Eirene, including even perhaps the curved passageway beneath the steps (though no evidence attests to such a corridor in St. Sophia). Somewhere in front of the *synthronon* stood a ciborium "reared on fourfold arches of silver" resting on silver columns, with an octagonal pyramidal canopy of silver towering over the altar table (*mensa*) and adorned with acanthus, topped by a silver orb and finally a cross.[119] Resting upon a gold slab, the altar table was also made of gold embellished with semiprecious stones. It was covered with a silk and gold embroidery bearing images of Christ between Peter and Paul standing in a tripartite arcade, the miracles of Christ, and charitable deeds of Justinian.[120]

The *bema*, enclosing, it seems, most of the floor area beneath the eastern half-dome, was rectangular in shape and fenced off by an open barrier but accessible by three doors. It was composed of variegated marble parapet slabs held in place by twelve silver-covered columns carrying an architrave bearing images of angels, apostles, the Virgin, and Christ and many lamps.[121] The parapet slabs carried monograms of the emperor and his deceased consort, Theodora. All or most of the *bema* was covered with silver sheets.

Projecting westward from the bema was the *solea* (corresponding to the western *schola cantorum*), a raised pathway reserved for members of the clergy which was bordered by parapets of marble slabs secured by small piers. The *solea* led to the *ambo*, on which the poet Paul lavishes particular attention.[122] The *ambo* was positioned on the longitudinal axis of the church, somewhere east of the center of the nave. Eight "cunningly wrought" columns supporting gilded capitals rose to support a circular or oval platform high enough for cantors to stand beneath it and intone chants. Constructed of marble and ivory, the platform was accessible by two flights of stairs, one at the east and one at the west. The entire ambo was encircled by a fence of eight larger columns with marble slabs sheathed in silver between them, and these columns and their gilded carved capitals supported an architrave designed with gilded ivy leaves on a blue ground and bearing a cross and lamps.[123] Paul likened the "tower-like ambo...adorned with its meadows of marble" to an island rising from the sea of the nave and joined to the mainland sanctuary by an isthmus, "beaten by waves on either side."[124]

A *metatorium* or screened-off place was installed somewhere in the south aisle; its exact location has not been fixed with certainty. It enclosed a throne for the emperor to hear the gospels on holy feast days.[125] Since Theodora had died about fifteen years before the second inauguration of the church, Paul the Silentiary has no need to specify a place for her in the second church. He indicates, however, that the place for women was in the galleries of the second church, but his statement has been questioned.[126] Indeed, many details of the enfolding of the liturgy of the Eucharist in the church of Justinian remain unclear.[127]

It is safe to assume that not only were the general lines of the furnishings described by the poet Paul rooted in local liturgical practice, but that also they were designed on a much larger scale and were far more costly than those of all earlier church buildings in the city. The furnishings of the second church of Justinian apparently remained in place until the Crusaders sacked the church in 1204. After the Crusaders left Constantinople in 1261 the furnishings were restored under the emperor Michael Palaeologus. When the eastern portion of the central dome of the church fell down in 1346 some of them were again destroyed. These the empress Anna, wife of the emperor Andronicus Palaeologus, subsequently restored. This set of fittings remained in tact until the Sultan Mehmet Fatih seized control of St. Sophia in 1453 and replaced them by a mihrab.[128]

Given the hugeness of St. Sophia it is not surprising that its staff was sizeable. A law of 535 announces that no further clergy were to be appointed until the staff had fallen to 60 priests, 100 male deacons, 40 female deacons, 90 subdeacons, 110 readers, 25 singers, and 100 custodians and porters.[129] Although these persons had to serve three other neighboring churches, their numbers reflect the central critical importance of the cathedral in the religious life of the city.

THE BUILDING MATERIALS

The masons of Justinian's St. Sophia used stone, bricks, and mortar, in contrast to the concrete common in monuments

of the Roman Empire in the West. Whereas earlier structures in Constantinople, including presumably the pre-
Justinianic St. Sophia, were constructed of mortared rubble
work or the regular alternation of one or more courses of
stone with a number of brick courses, the new St. Sophia
uses stone principally in the piers and regularly coursed
bricks and mortar for the walls.[130] No exposed brick walls
reveal a fill of roughly coarsed rubble.[131] The stone is either
limestone or greenstone.[132] The columns and the three cornices of the interior consist of marble. Iron was used for
the cramps between adjacent blocks of stone in the cornices and for long tie bars spanning across the springings of
arches and vaults, or between the walls of the buttress piers
between above the gallery roofs. Lead sheets varying in size
and thickness protect the outer surfaces of the vaults and
dome, and they are reported to have been laid in the four
main piers.[133] Bronze was used for the sheathings of all the
doorways opening into and from the inner narthex and for
the casing of the central doorway (the so-called Imperial
Door) leading from the inner narthex to the nave.[134] No-
ticeably absent is the use of timber, except in a small amount
as ties and as the backing of the bronze doors.

The entire edifice was entirely covered with masonry
vaults of different types and constructed of bricks embedded in thick beds of mortar: the central dome, the two half-
domes, the semidomes, barrel vaults, and domical vaults over
the ground-floor aisles and galleries, all constructed of
pitched bricks and thick mortar beds and masterly varied to
meet the particular requirements of the case.[135] The mortar
bed joints are thicker (50 to 60 mm.) than the bricks in a
proportion of about 3:2, so that the structure consists of a
greater mass of mortar than brick. Nearly all the bricks av-

erage about 0.375 m. square and 40 to 50 mm. thick, but the principal arches beneath the central dome were constructed with unusually large bricks up to 0.7 m. square; presumably they were imported.[136] Remarkably the central dome (including ribs) measures only 80 cm. just above the crown of the window arches and gradually diminishes toward the point where the ribs are merged within the web, where the total thickness is only about 65 cm.[137] The main half-domes are slightly less than 0.8 m. thick, perhaps constructed of two regularly-sized bricks.

Justinian's new churches of the Holy Apostles and St. Eirene in Constantinople, also constructed after the Nika revolt of 532, were likewise altogether covered by masonry vaults. By contrast, the church of SS. Peter and Paul located in the Hormisdas Palace near the Sea of Marmara that was built by Justinian as early as 518/ 519, while "crown prince" during the reign of his uncle Justin I (518-27), was a traditional wooden-roof basilica, as presumably had been all earlier basilican church buildings in the capital.[138] The great Justinianic foundations of St. Sophia, St. Eirene, and the Holy Apostles in Constantinople, as well as the church of St. John the Evangelist at Ephesus and others which he had rebuilt after the Nike revolt, antedate by over six centuries the first completely vaulted basilican church buildings of the Romanesque period in western Europe. Like the Romanesque basilicas of France, Spain, Germany, and Norman England, Justinian's St. Sophia was designed to be a far more fireproof edifice than had been its predecessor. The destruction wrought by the city fires of the Nika riot must surely be counted as one of the principal reasons for the widespread introduction of masonry vaulting in Constantinopolitan church building during the reign of Justinian. So Agathias writes that in Justinian's St. Sophia "the use of wood (was) avoided in order to prevent it from ever being easily set on fire again."[139]

RELATED MONUMENTS

A very close comparison to the conception of Justinian's St. Sophia is the neighboring church of SS. Sergius and Bacchus, also built by the emperor, in the Palace of Hormisdas, located either to the north or the south side of the aforementioned basilican church of SS. Peter and Paul, with which it shared atrium, forecourt, and propylaea. Today it is known as the Little St. Sophia (Küçük Ayasofya Camii).[140] Like Justinian's St. Sophia, SS. Sergius and Bacchus is a two-storied construction, in this case a central plan, with an octagon placed inside an irregularly shaped rectangular enclosure pierced by a single projecting apse to the east and a single narthex to the west (Fig. 11). The inner octagonal shell is covered by a sophisticated "pumpkin dome" of sixteen alternately straight and concave segments, without a cornice or pendentives, but with a window placed at the base of each of its eight straight sides. It is generally assumed that this is the original dome of the church, but Mainstone has recently questioned this.[141] (The continued use of the building as a mosque has prevented excavation and structural examination of the monument.) The inner octagonal shell consists of alternating straight sides and curved columnar exedrae in two stories, with a pair of columns in the galleries set directly above the pair on the ground floor. If this church were bisected and each half made to flank opposite sides of a domed cubic core space, the design would roughly approximate that of St. Sophia.

Fig 11. SS. Sergius and Bacchus, Constantinople. Interior to east (Müller-Wiener)

It is sometimes asserted that SS.Sergius and Bacchus served as the precursor of Justinian's St. Sophia, even that Anthemius of Tralles was its architect.[142] Neither statement can be substantiated. The long epigram carved on the entablature of SS. Sergius and Bacchus refers to both emperor Justinian and his empress, the God-crowned Theodora, and the carved melon capitals in the church bear monograms of this imperial couple.[143] Since Justinian was crowned emperor and Theodora empress in the year 527, the church could date that early, as is often stated.[144] But a written document dated to 536 mentions a priest of the church named Paul when Justinian and Theodora were the reigning monarchs who attended a church council, thus establishing a terminus ante quem of that year.[145] In short, SS. Sergius and Bacchus has to be viewed as a contemporary rather than an antecedent of St. Sophia.

The differences between these two church buildings are instructive. The variance in their scale is enormous, and functionally they are dissimilar. Originally squeezed in between two pre-existing edifices, SS. Sergius is a central-plan edifice, whose dome measures about 17 m. in diameter, whereas St. Sophia a free-standing expanded domed basilica. Yet the two church buildings are altogether covered by masonry vaults. And while both are covered by a central dome, the present dome of St. Sophia sits on a cornice supported by four pendentives, as conceivably was true of its first dome; cornice and pendentives are absent in SS. Sergius and Bacchus. More significantly, the dome of St. Sophia is flanked and structurally supported at least to some extent by two spacious half-domes to the east and west. In both buildings the double-storied walls between the piers are alternately straight and curved, but in SS. Sergius and Bacchus the columns of the two stories are aligned, in contradistinction to the unclassical disposition of supports in St. Sophia. In the former the lower story is trabeated and only the galleries are arcuated, but in St. Sophia both orders are arcuated. In St. Sophia two entablatures—a gallery cornice and an upper cornice—wrap around the nave, while in the smaller church there is one cornice which stops short of the sanctuary, and it bears a dedicatory inscription.[146] And the carved capitals differ in type.

Another building which has been adduced as an antecedent of Justinian's St. Sophia is the church of the third-century soldier martyr St. Polyeuktos at Constantinople, erected by the millionaire princess Anicia Juliana, the last descendent of the former Imperial House, a devout Christian, and a truly great Byzantine patroness of the arts. Her church of St. Polyeuktos had long been known from an epigram preserved in the *Anthologia Palatina* I.10, which records in seventy-six lines the foundation epigram placed around the nave of the church and outside its narthex by the patroness herself.[147] In 1960 architectural fragments from the foundation epigram turned up at the site known as Saraçhane, which Ihor Ševčenko immediately recognized and published with Cyril Mango.[148] This discovery led Martin Harrison four years later to begin excavating at Saraçhane, and he uncovered the surviving substructures of St. Polyeuktos; in 1986 Harrison in collaboration with other scholars issued his final report.[149] Although Mango, Ševčenko, and Harrison and his collaborators have assigned the church to the years 524 to 527, recent studies re-interpret brick stamps found by Harrison to indicate that construction of the church was begun as early as the years 509-11 and was brought to completion as early as 518.[150] Whatever its exact date, Anicia Juliana's St. Polyeuktos is clearly pre-Justinianic.

St. Polyeuktos was the largest, most ambitious, and most resplendent church in all of Constantinople before Justinian's St. Sophia. It was large (52 m. square), excluding its projecting apse and narthex—in other words, two-thirds the size of Justinian's St. Sophia. This big church was pre-

ceded by a paved atrium some 5 meters lower than the
church itself and narrower than it, and a broad staircase
would have led from the atrium to the church along its main
axis. Some walls excavated to the north of the atrium have
been identified as contemporary with the church and belonging to Anicia Juliana's palace. If her residence was situated in this place, the church of St. Polyeuktos was intended
to serve as her private "imperial" palace church. The foundation epigram and church remains also seem to make a
deliberate and explicit political statement which was both
imperial and dynastic.[151] The selection of Polyeuktos af-
firmed her descent from the emperor Theodosius II, whose
wife Eudocia had built an earlier church in honor of this
martyr, which the epigram confirms. The size and splendor
of the archaeological remains of the church can be inter-
preted as aristocratic and imperial.[152] Moreover, Harrison
has plausibly argued that the architect of Anicia Juliana's
church had in mind the Temple of Solomon in Jerusalem
while planning and executing it. The poem inscribed in the
church claimed that she "alone had conquered time and
surpassed the wisdom of the celebrated Solomon, raising a
temple to receive God." [153]

   Since the superstructure of the church is lost, a reconstruction of its layout and structural system is conjectural.
The lofty substructures contain two broad and deep foundation walls (8 m. by 6 m.) running east-west, and these elements suggested to Harrison that the church was vaulted
and featured a center bay covered by a hemispherical dome
18.5 m. on a side sitting on four broad arches rising from four
piers.[154] He conjectures that the dome rose as high as 34 m.
above the pavement of the nave, that it may have been supported by pendentives carrying a circular cornice (no archeological remnants of which have been identified), and

that the nave bays to the west and to the east would have been covered by barrel vaults, not half-domes.[155] The poem describing the church mentions columns set upon columns, disclosing that it was of two stories, with the columns in both stories lined up. The remnants of carved marble niches with frontal peacocks, their feathers outstretched—astonishing elements indeed, suggest that the interior featured at least four curved columnar exedrae.

The evidence for the presence of a dome over the center of the church is highly suggestive but in the last analysis circumstantial. The gigantic substructures of St. Polyeuktos do not necessarily sustain such a reconstruction. They admit of other possibilities that deserve mention. We know relatively little about the substructures of other Byzantine churches in Constantinople; those of St. Sophia have been examined only in part and those of SS. Sergius and Bacchus not at all.[156] Since St. Polyeuktos was constructed on sloping terrain, its massive substructures could have been laid out as part of a high podium on which the entire church stood, rather than as foundations for a particular set of piers and columns.[157] Or they could belong to a constructional system to facilitate the runoff of rainwater or to provide stability in case of earthquakes, which have been numerous at Constantinople.[158]

An alternative reconstruction has also been offered for St. Polyeuktos: a galleried "domed basilica" composed of two, not three, major bays—a short barrel-vaulted entrance bay and a domed central bay, with a barrel-vaulted forechoir to the east terminating in an apse.[159] According to this reconstruction, the edifice would presumably have resembled the church of St. Eirene in Constantinople, as it was rebuilt by Justinian beginning in 532.[160] Both proposals envision vaulted aisles and galleries, so that in either case Anicia Juliana's church was completely covered by masonry vaults and a dome, as was Justinian's St. Sophia.

If St. Polyeuktos bore a domed superstructure, was its structural design a creative innovation in the early Byzantine church architecture of Constantinople, or was it derived from or strongly inspired by a pre-existing type? Stephen Hill's recent re-examination of the church buildings of the eastern half of the southern coastlands of Asia Minor offers plausible arguments for the existence of vaulted and domed basilicas in masonry as early as fifty years before the erection of St. Sophia.[161] Perhaps half a dozen church ruins were originally basilicas covered by a central dome in masonry, and these monuments date from the reign of the Isaurian emperor Zeno (474-91).[162] Three examples in this region stand out as prominent representatives of the building type. One is the so-called "Cupola Church" at Meryemlık in Cilicia, probably erected by Zeno.[163] Now lying in ruins, its plan is clear (Fig. 12). Preceded by a semi-

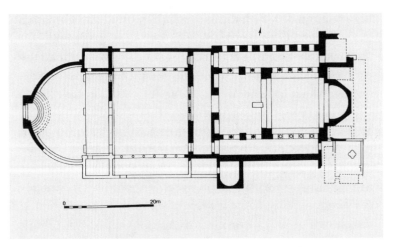

Fig 12. Meryemlık (Turkey). "Cupola church" (after Herzfeld and Guyer)

circular forecourt and a narthex to the west, it was a basilica (78 m. by 35 m.) composed of a wide nave in two bays and relatively narrow aisles carrying galleries. The aisles were definitely barrel vaulted in masonry, but it is a matter of dispute whether the west bay of the nave was surmounted by a barrel vault and the second bay (10.6 m. by 10.65 m.) by a masonry dome, or whether the west bay was covered by an ordinary wood roof and the second bay by a pyramidal tower construction. The former possibility now looms large.[164] Analogous church planning occurs in the later fifth-century East Church at Alahan in Isauria, an aisled basilican structure (now thought to have been a pilgrimage church rather than a monastery).[165] A basilica with galleries whose nave was divided into two bays, with the eastern bay oblong in shape, this church is smaller (23 m. by 15 m.) than the "Cupola Church" at Meryemlık. The roofing system of East Church at Alahan remains a matter of dispute. The east bay of its nave rose either in a pyramidal roof of timber or a dome of wood or stone carried by elegant squinch arches at the angles of the bay.[166] The system of roofing of this church remains a problem. A third closely related church is the "Domed Ambulatory Church" at Dağ Pazarı in Cilicia, also attributed to the reign of the emperor Zeno.[167] A church about 20 m. square (without the narthex), its central bay was probably covered by a masonry dome about 7.5 m. in diameter which was carried by piers 2.2 m. thick and apparently buttressed by the masonry barrel vaults over the side aisles of the edifice.[168] Early Byzantine domes in masonry on a small scale are recorded in Cilicia and Isauria as early as the fourth and certainly in the fifth century, and a stone dome on pendentives is firmly documented in the late fifth or early sixth century at Akkale in eastern Cilicia.[169] Rather than Meryemlık, Alahan, and Dağ Pazarı representing variants of purely hypothetical imperial models in Constantinople, it seems to me more likely that their type was exported from the eastern half of the south coastlands of Asia Minor to the capital where they were adapted and exploited in several decades before the reign of Justinian. Anicia Juliana's large church is the earliest example of the type in the capital.[170] Given the homeland of the two architects of Justinian's St. Sophia and the experimental nature of their design for his church, this interpretation of the evidence certainly deserves serious attention. Since no domed basilicas are recorded in ruins or written sources among the fifth-century churches of Constantinople, or Rome or Antioch in Syria for that matter, the Isaurian and Cilician examples of the last quarter of the fifth century must be reckoned with as at least one of the principal direct forerunners of the documented domed basilicas in sixth-century Constantinople and elsewhere in Byzantium. Isaurian builders were, moreover, known for their expertise in the construction of masonry buildings domes and vaults, and were hired by Justinian to repair the dome of St. Sophia in Constantinople after it collapsed in 558.[171]

Another type of church building with which Justinian's church should be closely associated, let me stress, is the double-shell quatrefoil. We know of about twenty double-shell quatrefoil buildings, and they are geographically widespread, extending from Italy and Egypt to the Balkans, Turkey (but not Constantinople), Syria, Armenia and Azerbaijan.[172] Although variations occur in the design of these monuments, all are marked by a quatrefoil center space surrounded by ambulatories, in some cases surmounted by galleries. The center space is marked off at the corners by piers, and from the straight sides project curved columnar exedrae which in the double-storied examples of the build-

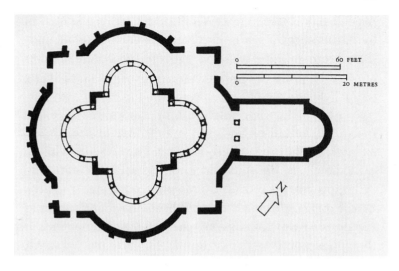

Fig 13. Seleucia Pieria (Turkey). Church, ground plan (after Krautheimer)

ing type are repeated at gallery level. Sometimes the perimeter walls or outer shell of the edifice echo the inner quatrefoil shell, in other cases they are rectilinear. The earliest datable example is the church of San Lorenzo at Milan which was originally built sometime in the third quarter of the fourth century and remodeled in the eleventh and sixteenth centuries.[173] But this type of building did not originate in Italy. The presence of galleries in fourth-century San Lorenzo points to a model somewhere in the eastern Mediterranean. Although some scholars reconstruct a masonry or even timber dome over San Lorenzo's center space, a square 23.8 m. on a side, I have argued elsewhere that the center of the original church was covered by a masonry groin vault.[174] Another double-shell quatrefoil lies in ruins at Perge in Pamphylia on the south coast of Turkey and may date as early as, or possibly earlier, than San Lorenzo.[175]

A good half-dozen double-shell quatrefoils are known in Syria and were built from the later fifth century to the mid-sixth century. Some if not most were cathedral churches and served as the headquarters of metropolitans reporting to the Patriarchate of Antioch, the capital of early Byzantine Syria.[176] The late fifth-century example at Seleucia Pieria, the harbor of ancient Antioch, may be the earliest example of the type in Syria (Fig. 13). The cathedral church of SS. Sergius, Bacchus and Leontius at Bosra, dating to 512/13, provides a second example in Syria. Although the quatrefoils at Seleucia Pieria and Bosra may have been covered by square pyramidal roofs constructed of timber rather than domes of masonry or timber, their curved columnar exedrae were covered by half-domes probably of stone masonry. Hence, these monuments, like San Lorenzo at Milan, provide a material source of inspiration for St. Sophia's scheme of a central dome flanked on two opposite sides by half-domes. By contrast, the quatrefoil cathedral at Apamea in Syria incorporated four massive piers from an earlier Roman edifice which may have supported a masonry dome. This church seems to date to 529, three years before Justinian began rebuilding St. Sophia.[176a] The now destroyed church known as St. Sophia at Adrianople in Thrace (modern Edirne at the western border of Turkey) may have served as the local cathedral (Fig. 14). Known from two rough sketch plans by Auguste Choisy and a single photograph of 1888, this St. Sophia was an important monument.[177] An aisled tetraconch, it was cross-shaped and of two stories, with a central core 15.5 m. on a side from which projected four arms 15.5 m. by 8.5 m. A dome about 14 m. in diameter originally covered the church and was probably constructed of brick; it collapsed at some unknown date in the Byzantine period, and the church was rebuilt with a fenestrated drum and a dome

Fig 14. Adrianople (modern Edirne, Turkey). "St. Sophia."
(after Mavrodinov, 1948)

half the size of the original one, the supporting piers being considerably thickened. The date of the first (and the rebuilt) church is conjectural. It is usually dated in the sixth century on the basis of its masonry as seen in a photograph of 1888; its exact date remains unknown, all trace of the church having disappeared.

Some of these aisled quatrefoil churches, especially those in the Balkans and Asia Minor, but perhaps not that in Milan, may have been known firsthand to Anthemius and Isidore the Elder, and the highly idiosyncratic design of these quatrefoils composed of a nuclear square bay enveloped by ancillary spaces may have provided one driving source for the experimentation and innovative planning of Justinian's architects, who, we have seen, imposed centralizing and verticalizing axes upon the traditional horizontal basilican layout established by the old St. Sophia and other early

Byzantine church buildings at Constantinople. Since the preponderance of these aisled quatrefoils served as cathedrals—and some of them, it seems, also as metropolitan church buildings, they would have provided appropriate functional as well as formal founts of inspiration for the engineer-architects of Justinian's new cathedral. For me this point is of some importance and has not been emphasized in this manner before.

JUSTINIAN'S SECOND DOME

Surely knowledgeable about the structural systems and functions of a large number of distantly related monuments, Anthemius and Isidore the Elder decided to erect a central dome exactly one hundred Byzantine feet in diameter over the emperor's new cathedral.[178] With their firm grasp of geometry the architects planned the great church with the utmost precision, but major difficulties developed when construction reached the springing of the four great arches. These difficulties are poignantly recounted by Procopius, twenty years after the fact.[179] The main piers began to tilt outward while the great eastern arch was going up; today the inclination of the piers from the vertical is almost 61 cm. (Fig. 8). Slow-hardening mortar was one of the causes of these tilts and deformations. Inadequate foundations for the main piers and buttressing were others. Concomitantly, the great north and south arches exerted enough pressure on the subjacent tympanums that some columns—either those in the tympanums or those in the galleries, began to shed flakes. Anthemius and Isidore referred the problems to the emperor who, according to Procopius, advised them how to solve them: complete construction of the great arch.[180] The masons carried out the emperor's suggestion, "sealing by experiment the truth of his idea."[181] While the constructional crises may have been temporarily solved— projections were added to the main and buttress piers at both ground and gallery levels, the structural deformations persisted.[182] The original dome may have been planned as a perfect circle, but it was actually constructed as an ellipse about 1.98 m. wider from north to south than from east to west because of the outward settlement of the main and buttress piers. These and other deformations continued until the collapse of the first dome, and even after the dome was rebuilt by Isidore the Younger (its major axis is 2.55 m. longer than its minor axis), so that today the building is the most structurally deformed building in the western world after the Leaning Tower of Pisa.[183]

Masonry domes of considerable span had of course been constructed prior to Justinian's reign.[184] That of the second-century Hadrianic Pantheon at Rome is the most celebrated. Springing from a circular wall 6 m. thick, the dome of the Pantheon is built of structural concrete, is hemispherical in shape, and has a span of 43.3 m., the largest built up to that time.[185] It remained unmatched until 1446 when Brunelleschi designed the dome of the cathedral of Florence and 1590 when construction of Michelangelo's dome for St. Peter's (whose span is 42.5 m.) at Rome was finally brought to completion. Only in late nineteenth-century Paris was the span of the Pantheon's dome substantially surpassed through the employment of metal-framed structures, and this century when reinforced concrete roof shells were constructed, such as that of the Centre National des Industries et des Techniques built in Paris in 1958 with a span of 219 m.[186]

Interpretations of the complex structure of St. Sophia were begun by Auguste Choisy in the nineteenth century, but a far more fundamental contribution to a general structural assessment of the fabric was made by Rowland Mainstone in the 1960s, and his work forms the basis of subsequent structural studies.[187] More recently, a team of engineers at Princeton University headed by Robert Mark has scientifically examined the domes of the Pantheon at Rome and of St. Sophia at Constantinople by the use of three-dimensional finite-element computer modeling to determine how forces are distributed within the fabric of these domes.[188] Still underway, the Princeton project has shown that the Pantheon's concrete dome is not as monolithic as previously thought, and that its base experienced meridional cracking owing to tensile stresses that would have been accentuated by the curing of newly cast concrete and also by environmental gradients, such as changes in the temperature caused by rain storms. Mark is convinced that Anthemius and Isidore the Elder were familiar with the cracking in the lower portions of the Pantheon's dome, but this I seriously doubt. The actual construction of the Pantheon is not exposed internally. The whole of its drum and most of its dome are sheathed with ornamental architecture. Unless the anonymous architect of the Pantheon recorded the structure of the monument in writing or in drawings and this material fell into the hands of the Byzantines, the structural engineering of the Pantheon's dome remained unknown at Constantinople. Whereas the whole of the dome of St. Sophia is composed solely of brick and mortar, construction of the that of the Pantheon involved the use of various filling materials most carefully graded: travertine, tufa, brick and a light volcanic pumice in the upper portion of the dome. Neither of St. Sophia's engineer- ar-

chitects is known to have visited Rome. It is true that
Anthemius had a brother residing in Rome, but he was a
physician rather than a *mechanikos* and is not known to have
had any interest in architecture. The Pantheon had no prog-
eny at Rome, and no masonry dome is known to have been
constructed in the city in the period from about the year
350 to the age of Justinian.[189] The historical and archeological record precludes the possibility of St. Sophia standing
in the shadow of the city of Rome.

Justinian's engineer-architects were surely familiar with
domed buildings in the eastern Mediterranean, not only the
masonry domes and masonry domes on pendentives in the
eastern half of southern Asia Minor but also elsewhere in
Asia Minor, the provinces to the west of Constantinople,
and at Constantinople itself.[190] The Temple of Asklepios
Soter at Pergamon in northwest Turkey, erected just before
the middle of the second century A.D., is a niched rotunda
with a drum built of fine ashlar and a dome (23.85 m. in
diameter) of kiln-dried brick, laid radially and reinforced
at the spring by an outer ring of mortared rubble.[191] This
may mark the beginning of the use of brick as a vaulting
material in Asia Minor.[192] The earliest recorded example in
Asia Minor of a pendentive dome covering a rectangular
space is the mausoleum in the eastern necropolis at Side in
Pamphylia. This is a small structure (12.50 m. by 10.55 m.)
whose construction is ascribed to the first half of the fifth
century A.D.[193] This edifice is designed with quarter-domes
over the niches expanding from the core space (6.25 m. by
5.35 m.), and the pendentives (still standing in part) are constructed of radially rather than horizontally laid bricks. This
technique of brick construction occurs at Side as early as
the third century A.D. Although quite small in scale, this
"East Mausoleum" of Side provides a closer forerunner to

the system of a central dome on pendentives and two half-domes in St. Sophia than does that of the Pantheon.[194]

For a surviving example of a brick dome on a monumental scale in the eastern Mediterranean the Rotunda of Galerius at Thessaloniki in northern Greece needs to be adduced. Originally built around 300 A.D., the Rotunda consists of a cylindrical wall 6.25 m. thick carrying a hemispherical dome with a diameter of 24.15 m.[195] This dome has an intrados of bricks laid radially, several bricks thick and backed, at any rate up to a certain height, with mortared rubble. While construction of the dome was left unfinished upon the death of Galerius in 311, it was brought to completion when the edifice was converted into a Christian church (and the splendid mosaics put up), most probably in the mid-fifth century.[196] Although Thessaloniki lies in a seismic zone—as recently as 1978 the city was struck by an earthquake measuring 6.2 on the Richter scale, the dome of the Rotunda has never collapsed, even though it exhibits extensive meridional cracks which have been tracked by modern Greek specialists. Surely a contributing reason for its survival virtually intact to the present day is because its late Roman master builder took precautions in its design. The lower (Galerian) part of the dome, to a height of 7 m. is a segment of a hemisphere based on a center on the level of the springing line, while the upper part (mid-fifth century) has a different curvature, based on a center about 2 m. higher. By this means the late Roman masons were able to reduce the effective span from 24.15 m. (or 24.5 m.), corbeling the lower part inwards without scaffolding and making the pitch of the crown less dangerously shallow.[197] If Anthemius and Isidore the Elder had taken such precautions some eighty years later, their dome for Justinian's church—whatever its original configuration was—may not have collapsed in 558, even though its span is substantially

greater than that of the Rotunda. But they may not have
been familiar with the constructional means of the latter's
dome since its structure was completely sheathed by Christian mosaics long before their time. When fully intact, these
mosaics would have made the change of curvature difficult
to discern from the floor of the Rotunda.

Whether other sizeable domes in the eastern Mediterranean, such as that of the roughly contemporary St. Sophia at
Adrianople (Fig. 14) incorporated such a precaution we simply do not know. But it should be noted that in Roman and
Early Byzantine times mortared brick rather than concrete
was the standard building material in the Aegean and Asia
Minor, including Constantinople, and Justinian's engineer-
architects came from southwest Asia Minor. It takes too great
a leap of faith to assume, without any documentation, that
they had become cognizant of the cracks in the dome of the
Pantheon and translated its graded concrete material into
the standard building material of Justinian's capital.

While the dome of St. Sophia was not modeled on that of
the Pantheon at Rome, Robert Mark and his colleagues have
been informing us more fully of the structural properties of
both brick and concrete domes than has been known in the
past. Mark has also made a collateral observation that merits
mention. The ring of forty windows around the base of the
second dome of Justinian's church, which may repeat the
number of windows in the first dome, was not designed audaciously, solely for visual effect, creating, as it does, the illu-
sion of a diaphanous floating dome, suspended from heaven
by a golden chain, as it was put by one contemporary writer,
quoting Homer's vision of Zeus suspending the whole earth
from Mount Olympus in the *Iliad*.[198] It was also designed to
avoid the kind of meridional cracking experienced by the
Pantheon and, I would add to Mark, masonry domes in the

Eastern Mediterranean with which Justinian's engineer-architects would have been familiar. Whether such a factor also accounts for the five windows near the base of each of St. Sophia's two large half-domes depends on whether Anthemius and Isidore the Elder anticipated that they too would develop cracks, as indeed they did.

But this consideration of engineering could not have been the only reason for the provision of the windows in the dome (and half-domes). A central dome provided with windows had been built over churches earlier in the eastern Mediterranean, and such a central crowning source of light had before been associated with the divine and the illuminated dome as a dwelling place of divinity. Gregory of Nazianzus, who had served as bishop of Constantinople (380-381) before assuming the bishopric of Nazianzus (382-384), near Caesarea in Asia Minor, describes the central covering of the octagonal martyrial church of his father (who had also been bishop of Nazianzus) as follows: "At the top is a gleaming heaven that illuminates the eye all round with abundant founts of light—truly a place wherein light dwells."[199] He is describing a dome with a corona of windows. As I have suggested above, a fenestrated dome admitting light associated with the divine may have been a tradition adapted in Justinian's program for St. Sophia.

CONCLUSION

Procopius provides us with his eyewitness perspective on how the sixth-century worshiper-spectator was affected by Justinian's first St. Sophia:

> Whenever one goes to the church to pray, one realizes at
> once that it is not by human power or skill, but by divine

influence that this church has been so wonderfully built. The visitor's mind is lifted up on high to God, feeling that he cannot be far away but must love to dwell in this place He himself has chosen. All this does not happen only when one sees the church for the first time, but the same thing occurs to the visitor on each successive occasion, as if the sight were ever a new one. No one has ever had a surfeit of this spectacle, but when persons are present in the building men rejoice in what they see, and when they are away from it, they take delight in talking of it.[200]

Justinian's St. Sophia is in every sense of the word a great church. Its contemporaries regarded it as "like no other in the world" (*singulariter in mundo*).[201] Its first two engineer-architects experimented with concepts and designs known to them firsthand and from written and diagrammatic accounts of monuments at various if not indeed countless localities in order to create an adventuresome fabric of stunning novelty and daring audacity, far surpassing any church building that had been erected anywhere before. This latter characterization of Justinian's church is borne out by Procopius and Paul the Silentiary. While a few salient aspects of its planning seem to have been prompted by the edifice at the site before the Nika riot, its finished layout bears no relationship to that of its predecessor, nor can it be said to have genetically evolved from any other source or set of models. If the church has been here discussed in terms of other buildings, the aim has been to demonstrate that its structure and design were *sui generis* rather than derivative. Earlier concepts and forms were examined by Anthemius and Isidore the Elder, but a select number of them were chosen and creatively transfigured so as to manifest tangibly and visibly the power, prestige, and aims of their patron. The result was a landmark in the history of world architecture, and recognized as such in its own day.

Notes

1. J. B. Bury, "The Nika Riot," *Journal of Hellenic Studies* 17 (1897), pp. 92ff., remains the fundamental account of the riot. Cf. A. Cekalova, *Konstantinopel' v VI-om veke, Vosstanie Nika v 532 godu* (Moscow, 1986). For a modern assessment of Bury's study, consult M. Jeffreys, "Bury, Malalas and the Nika Riot," in *The Sixth Century: End or Beginning?* Ed. P. Allen and E. Jeffreys (Brisbane, 1996), pp. 42ff. The principal historical sources are Procopius, *Wars* I.24; John Malalas, *Chronicle* XVIII.473ff. (*The Chronicle of John Malalas*, trans. E. Jeffreys et al [Melbourne, 1986], pp. 251ff., 281ff. with valuable commentary); *Chron. pasch.* (*Chronicon Paschale 284-628 A.D.*(trans. M. Whitby and M. Whitby [Liverpool, 1989]), pp. 112, with highly instructive commentary and notes, especially on topography; Theophanes, *Chronographia* [ed. C. De Boor, Leipzig, 1883-85], p. 181; Marcellinus *comes, Chron., sub. a.* (*The Chronicle of Marcellinus*, trans. B. Croke [Sydney, 1995], p. 44).

2. The *Chronicon Paschale s.a. 532* (*ed.cit.*, p. 117) reports that the "whole of the Great Church together with its awesome and marvelous columns was completely demolished on all four sides."

3. For Theodora's speech: Procopius, *Wars* I.24.33-34. Averil Cameron, *Procopius and the Sixth Century* (Berkeley, 1985), p. 69, warns us not to take the speech at face value.

4. John the Lydian, *De Mag.* III, 70, gives the figure of 50,000, while John Malalas, *Chronicle* 476 (trans. Jeffreys et al, *Chronicle of John Malalas,* p. 280), says it was 35,000.

5. J. R. Martindale, *The Prosopography of the Later Roman Empire*, vol. 3A (Cambridge, 1992), p. 88 (Anthemius II) and p. 724 (Isidorus 4).

6. G. Downey, "Byzantine Architects: Their Training and Methods," *Byzantion* 18 (1946-48), pp. 99ff.

7. Agathias, *The Histories* V.6.3, ed. J. D. Frendo (Berlin, 1975), p. 141.

8. Agathias, *The Histories* V.6.7-8.6, ed. Frendo, pp. 141ff., provides a detailed account of Anthemius using mechanical tricks with steam pipes and mirrors to make the life of a neighbor named Zeno miserable.

9. T. L. Heath, *A Manual of Greek Mathematics* (London, 1931), p. 519; G. L. Huxley, *Anthemius of Tralles* (Cambridge, Mass., 1959).

10. No historical source confirms the often repeated speculation that Anthemius designed the Justinianic church of SS. Sergius and Bacchus in Constantinople: e.g., J. B. Bury, *History of the Later Roman Empire from the Death of Theodosius I. To the Death of Justinian (A.D. 395-565)* (London, 1923), vol. 2, p. 49; R. J. Mainstone, "The Structure of the Church of St. Sophia, Istanbul," *Transactions of the Newcomen Society* 38 (1965-66), p. 43.. Cf. A. E. Henderson, "SS. Sergius and Bacchus, Constantinople," *The Builder*, January 6, 1906, p. 7 It is true that Agathias, *The Histories* V.6.6. (*ed.cit.*), relates that Anthemius was responsible for marvelous buildings and other devices in Constantinople and in many other places, but all these activities may have occurred subsequent to his work on St. Sophia. Once summoned to Constantinople by Justinian--the date is unrecorded, Anthemius spent the rest of his life there (Agathias, *loc.cit.*). On SS. Sergius and Bacchus, see *infra*, pp. 5off.

11. Procopius *De aed* II.3.7-14. Cf. B. Croke and J. Crow, "Procopius and Dara," *Journal of Roman Studies* 73 (1983), pp. 143ff. During the Persian siege a *mechanikos* named Theodorus was in Dara and designed a cross trench to deter the enemy from breaking into the city (Martindale, *Prosopography of the Later Roman Empire*, vol. 3B, p. 1249, no. 13 ("Theodorus 13"). This Theodorus is probably identical with Theodorus *mechanikos* whom the emperor sent to Jerusalem in 531 to build the New Church (Nea) honoring the Mother of God (*ibid.*).

12. The date of February 23, 532 is provided only in a late chronicle source and is therefore open to doubt: Leo grammaticus, *Chronographia*, ed. I. Bekker (Bonn, 1842), p. 126. This Leo was Symeon Logothete, a writer who published under several names in the middle of the tenth century. The date of the inauguration of the church on December 27, 537, is certain. See C. Mango, "Byzantine Writers on the Fabric of Hagia Sophia," in *Hagia Sophia from the Age of Justinian to the Present*, ed. R. Mark and A. Çakmak (Cambridge, 1992), pp. 41ff.

13. Kontakion 54, which is not dated, was first published by C. Trypanis, *Fourteen Early Byzantine Cantica* (Vienna, 1968), and translated into English for the first time by A. Palmer, "The Inauguration Anthem of Hagia Sophia in Edessa: A New Edition and Translation with Historical and Archeological Notes and a Comparison with a

Contemporary Constantinopolitan Kontakion," *Byzantine and Modern Greek Studies*, 12 (1988), pp. 137ff. Palmer dates the kontakion to the occasion of the second inauguration of the church of St. Sophia at Constantinople, in 562. See, however, J. H. Barkhuizen, "Romanos Melodos: On Earthquakes and Fires, " *Jahrbuch der Österreichischen Byzantinistik* 45 (1995), pp 1ff..

14. No historical source substantiates the surmise of E. H. Swift, *Hagia Sophia* (New York, 1940), p. 12, that Anthemius had been working on plans for a new St. Sophia for a year before the Nika riot.

15. Greek text with English translation in H. B. Dewing and G. Downey, *Procopius, De aedificiis* Loeb Classical Library, vol. 7 (London, 1940). For the date of "The Buildings," as well as a judicious assessment of it, see Cameron, *Procopius*, chapter 6, esp. p. 84.

16. *De aed* I.1.6-11.

17. For Monophysitism, W. H. C. Frend, *The Rise of the Monophysite Movement* (Cambridge, 1972); A. Kazhdan, "Monophysitism," *Oxford Dictionary of Byzantium*, ed. A. Kazhdan (Oxford, 1991), pp. 1398f.

18. As emphasized by D. J. Geanakoplos, *Interaction of the "Sibling" Byzantine and Western Cultures in the Middle Ages and Italian Renaissance (330-1600)* (New Haven, 1976), chapter 5 ("Church Construction and 'Caesaropapism' in East and West from Constantine to Justinian"), esp. p.129.

19. In the preface to *Novella* 6, issued after 534, and addressed to the patriarch of Constantinople, Justinian describes an ideal *symphonia* or harmony between church and state--a concord made possible because both patriarch (or Church) and emperor (or State) are instituted by the authority of God and both are contained within his Kingdom on earth (*Basileia*): Justinian, *Novella* VI, in R. Schoell, ed., *Corpus Iuris Civilis*, vol. 3, *Novellae* (Berlin, 1912), pp. 35-36; English translation and commentary by D J. Geanakoplos, *Byzantium: Church, State and Civilization Seen through Contemporary Eyes* (Chicago, 1984), pp. 136f. In reality, as Geanakoplos points out, Justinian exercised authority over all phases of church administration--from appointing patriarchs to ordination to deposing recalcitrant patriarchs.

20. As C. Mango, *Byzantine Architecture* (New York, 1978), p. 57, observes that the system of fortifications undertaken by Justinian represents continuation of work launched by the emperor Anastasius but on a much vaster and more comprehensive scale. For example, Procopius lists over 600 fortresses which Justinian constructed or restored in the Balkans alone. While such statements are difficult to assess, they underscore the focus of the emperor's building program.

21. *De aed* IV.1.17.

22. G. Downey, "Justinian as Builder," *Art Bulletin* 32 (1950), pp. 262ff.; J. Moorhead, *Justinian* (London, 1994), pp. 52ff.

23. *De aed* VI.7.14-16. Procopius reports that at Septum the emperor not only constructed a church in honor of the Theotokos at the "threshold of the empire" but also strengthened its Roman fort "destroyed by time" and provided it with a garrison of troops. In actuality Justinian intended to replace the Arian church building of the Vandals with an Orthodox one.

24. John of Ephesus, *Ecclesiastical History*, part II (ed. Nau), p. 482, cited by Bury, *History of the Later Roman Empire*, II, p. 371.

25. So Cameron, *Procopius*, p. 89, without citing the activity of John of Ephesus in western Asia Minor.

26. *Descr. S. Sophiae*, verse 673 (trans. C. Mango, *The Art of the Byzantine Empire, 312-1453* [Englewood Cliffs, 1972], p. 86). For the entire text of the encomium, see the edition of P. Friedländer, *Johannes von Gaza und Paulus Silentiarius* (Leipzig and Berlin, 1912). The English translation in W. R. Lethaby and H. Swainson, *The Church of Sancta Sophia, Constantinople* (London and New York) is incomplete and obsolete. See now Mango, *Art of the Byzantine Empire*, pp. 80ff., 91ff. For the poem see R. Macrides and P. Magdalino, "The Architecture of Ekphrasis: Construction and Context of Paul the Silentiary's Poem on Hagia Sophia," *Byzantine and Modern Greek Studies*, 12 (1988), pp. 47-82; M. Whitby, "The Occasion of Paul the Silentiary's *Ekphrasis* of S. Sophia," *Classical Quarterly*, n.s. 35 (1985), pp. 215-228.

27. Greek text quoted and translated by Geanakoplos, *Byzantium*, p. 131.

28. As suggested by R. J. Mainstone, *Hagia Sophia: Architecture, Structure and Liturgy of Justinian's Great Church* (New York, 1988), p. 145.

29. The *Diegesis* (Narration), ed. T. Preger, *Scriptores originum Constantinopolitanarum* (Leipzig, 1902), vol. I: 74-108. For the date of this account, G. Dagron, *Constantinople imaginaire* (Paris, 1984), pp. 265ff. For a partial translation into English, Mango, *Art of the Byzantine Empire*, pp. 96ff. See also the commentary by Mango on the value of this text in his "Byzantine Writers," pp. 45ff.

30. For the use of architectural plans and drawings in late antiquity, see Downey, 'Byzantine Architects," pp. 114ff. Unnoticed by Downey is the late antique building manual *De diversis fabricis architectonicae* which refers to three types of figures: the plan (*ichnographia*), the elevation (*orthographia*), and the perspective (*scenographia*): "tres figurae, ichnographia, orthographia, scenographia. Ichnographia est areae vel soli et fundamentorum descriptio, orthographia est laterum et altitudinis extructio. Scenographia est frontis et totius operis per picturam ostensis"

(H. Plommer, *Vitruvius and Later Roman Building Manuals* [Cambridge, 1973], p. 41). In this text these three types of figures are to be drawn up for a future building, hence part of the architect's brief for presentation to the patron. The language of this text is different than that of Vitruvius. It is possible that in designing St. Sophia Anthemius and Isidore the Elder used a system of square compartmentalization, like the Western medieval method of *quadratura* in general. The layout of Justinian's Church of the Holy Apostles in Constantinople is said by the tenth-century Byzantine poet Constantine of Rhodes in his description of the church (verses 549-558, 602-604) to have been designed on a cruciform system of five squares, as if the four vertical sides of a central cube had been lowered to earth radially round about it: E. Legrand, *Revue des études grecques* 9 (1896), pp. 32ff. See also Mainstone, *Hagia Sophia*, pp. 176ff.; W. Meyer-Christian, "Hagia Sophia, The Engineers Planning of Anthemios and Isidoros, Reconstruction," in *Domes from Antiquity to the Present. Proceedings of the IASS-MSU International Symposium, Istanbul, 1988* (Istanbul, 1988), pp. 173ff.

31.   *De aed* I.i.24.

32.   *Diegesis*, 9. For the contention that the eight porphyry columns came from the third-century Temple of the Sun in Rome, see Mango, "Byzantine Writers," p.46.

33.   *Ibid.*, on the private dwellings that had to be expropriated.

34.   For the construction of the Nea the administrative procedures are recorded by the sixth-century hagiographer Cyril of Scythopolis in his *Life of St. Sabas: Vitae Sabae*, ch. 73 (ed. E. Schwartz [Leipzig, 1939], pp. 176-78). Justinian assigned Theodorus *mechanikos* to construct the church (for this individual see n. 11 supra) and granted funds to Cyril of Scythopolis for the church. The tax clerks (*trakteutai*) of the office of the praetorian prefect in Palestine supplied the gold necessary to cover the costs. Peter, archbishop of Jerusalem, exercised final authority over the project, but Barachos, bishop of Bakatha, was charged with immediate oversight of the project. Procopius, *De aed* V.vi.1-26, reports in unusual detail about technical problems incurred during construction of the church. See also N. Avigad, "A Building Inscription of the Emperor Justinian and the Nea in Jerusalem," *Israel Exploration Journal* 27 (1977), pp. 145ff

35.   Theophanes, *Chronographia* a.m. 6030 (ed. C. De Boor [Leipzig, 1883-85], vol. 1).

36.   For the dedication in 360: *Chronicon pasch.* I.544 (trans. Mango, *Art of the Byzantine Empire*, p.26). See further in G. Dagron, *Naissance d'une capitale; Constantinople et les institutions de 330 à 451* (Paris, 1974), pp. 397ff. A

Constantinian date was maintained by R. Krautheimer, "The Ecclesiastical Building Policy of Constantine," in *Costantino il Grande dall'antíchità all'umanesimo.* Colloquio sul Christianesimo nel mondo antica, Macerata 18-20 Dicembre 1990, vol. 2 (Macerata, 1993), p. 548, n. 88.

37. For the evidence that the first St. Sophia was an aisled wooden-roofed basilica, consult A. M. Schneider, *Die Grabung im Westhof der Sophienkirche zu Istanbul* (Berlin, 1941); T. F.. Mathews, *The Early Churches of Constantinople: Architecture and Liturgy* (University Park, 1971), pp. 11ff.; Mainstone, *Hagia Sophia*, pp. 134ff. and fig. 165 (tentative reconstruction of the pre-Justinianic church). For the layout of the aisled basilica of the Holy Sepulcher compound at Jerusalem, see V. Corbo, *Il Santo Sepolcro a Gerusalemme*, 3 vols. (Jerusalem, 1981-82) and R. Krautheimer, *Early Christian and Byzantine Architecture*, 4th ed. rev. (Harmondsworth, 1986), pp. 60ff..

38. *Chronicon pasch.* (see note 1 *supra*); Theophanes, *Chronographia* (Migne, *Patrologia Graeca* 108, col. 425).

39. Palladius, *De vita S. Ioannis Chrysostomi* (Migne, *Patrologia Graeca* 47, cols. 35-36). The authorship of this vita is questionable.

40. John Chrysostom is said to have "come down to the church" from his episcopal palace to pray (*ibid.*).

41. Socrates, *H.E.* II.16 (Migne, *Patrologia Graeca* 67, col. 217); G. Downey, "The Name of the Church of St. Sophia in Constantinople," *Harvard Theological Review*, 52 (1959), pp. 37ff.; Averil Cameron, "Procopius and the Church of St. Sophia," *loc.cit.*, 58 (1965), pp. 161ff. J. Meyendorff, ""Wisdom-Sophia: Contrasting Approaches to a Complex Theme, " *Dumbarton Oaks Papers*, 41 (1987), pp. 391ff.

41A. See *Chronicon pasch.*, p. 585.

42. Schneider, *Grabung*, p. 6, thought that the portico was part of the main facade of the church as rebuilt by Theodosius II, but Mainstone, *Hagia Sophia*, pp. 135ff. correctly maintains that it must belong to the west wall of the atrium in front of the basilican church. J. B. Ward-Perkins, "Notes on the Structure and Building Methods of Early Byzantine Architecture," in *The Great Palace of the Byzantine Emperors, Second Report*, ed. D. T. Rice (Edinburgh, 1958), p. 64, suggests that the wall to the east of the portico belongs to the fourth-century church, an opinion shared by Krautheimer, "Ecclesiastical Building Policy," p. 548, n. 88.

43. If the nave and aisles were squarish in proportions, as were those of the martyrion basilica of the fourth-century Holy Sepulchre complex in Jerusalem, there would have been sufficient space for a narthex

interposed between the nave and aisles to the east and the atrium to the west. Similar planning marks the mid-fifth century basilica of St. John Studius (Imrahor Camii) at Istanbul, the city's earliest preserved church: W. Müller-Wiener, *Bildlexikon zur Topographie Istanbul* (Tübingen, 1977), pp. 147ff. To the north of the east wall of the present St. Sophia stands a domed circular structure known as the *skeuophylakion*, which served as a treasury (Mainstone, *Hagia Sophia*, pp. 137ff. and figs. 161-162; see also n. 96 *infra*). It dates from the original or the rebuilt church of Theodosius II and may mark approximately the east end of the original fourth-century church building.

44. Uttered by Stephen of Novgorod, a Russian pilgrim of the fourteenth century, as quoted by A. A. Vasiliev, *History of the Byzantine Empire, 324-1453* (Madison, 1964), I, p. 189.

45. For over three decades it was surveyed by the architect Robert L. Van Nice, who published two facsimiles of measured drawings: *St. Sophia in Istanbul: An Architectural Survey*, 2 vols. (Washington D.C., 1965 and 1986). Eleven of Van Nice's drawings have been republished in R. Mark and A. S. Çakmak, eds., *Hagia Sophia from the Age of Justinian to the Present* (Cambridge, 1992), pp. 228ff. The drawings of Van Nice accurately delineate general plans and the major horizontal and vertical sections and elevations and include two precise isometric views. They have enormously increased our understanding of the present and original fabrics of the church. But they fail to record many construction details and features of the present structural fabric, such as materials used, bonds and lack of bonds, and cracks and separations, in part because stretches of the working masonry were never open to view. And it is to be regretted that Van Nice never published his announced explanatory text. He did, however, issue a number of important preliminary reports: W. Emerson and R. L. Van Nice, "Hagia Sophia, Istanbul: Preliminary Report of a Recent Examination of the Structure," *American Journal of Archaeology*, 47 (1943), pp. 403ff., and notes 56, 77, 130, and 183 *infra*. Van Nice's drawings need to be supplemented by those of Mainstone, *Hagia Sophia*, which present a possible intended form of the church in the year 562, without any unintended deformations. Some of Mainstone's drawings are diagrammatic, showing the major changes he believes occurred during construction and later. Mainstone's work on the building covers thirty years, including several occasions in the 1960s when he collaborated with Van Nice. The critical importance of the contribution of Van Nice and Mainstone notwithstanding, major disagreements persists about the structure of the church in both 537 and 562. Some of them will be noted in these pages.

46. I borrow the term "expanded domed basilica" from S. Hill, *The Early*

Byzantine Churches of Cilicia and Isauria (Aldershot, 1996), p. 50, without trying to distort what I see as the loose relationship of Justinian's design for St. Sophia to related monuments (see *infra*).

47. The longitudinal axis of the church is not truly east-west but points approximately 33 degrees south of east. For descriptive purposes in these pages it is assumed to be east-west.

48. As demonstrated by Mathews, *Early Churches of Constantinople, passim*. For the west entrance system of St. Sophia and related Justinianic church buildings, see C. Strube, *Die westliche Eingangsseite der Kirchen von Konstantinopel in justinianischer Zeit: Architektonische und quellenkritische Untersuchungen* (Wiesbaden, 1973). In the late Byzantine period visitors of various nationalities mistakenly report that St. Sophia had 360 to 365 doors (one even claims 752 of them!): G. P. Majeska, *Russian Travelers to Constantinople in the Fourteenth and Fifteenth Centuries* (Washington, D.C., 1984), p. 235 and n. 190

49. They occur in Greece, for instance, in the five-aisled basilica at Kenchreai erected in the late fifth or sixth century: R. M. Rothaus, "The Kenchreai Basilica," *Abstracts of Papers, Twenty-First Annual Byzantine Studies Conference*, New York City (1995), p. 62.

50. Strube, *Die westliche Eingangsseite*, pp. 36ff., for the west facade. For marbles on the remainder of the exterior, possible, but not certain, see M. Restle, "Konstantinopel," *Reallexikon zur byzantinischen Kunst*, 4 (1989/90), col. 427.

51. Procopius, *De aed* I.i.28-29 (trans. Mango, *Art of the Byzantine Empire*, p. 74).

52. L. E. Butler, "Hagia Sophia's Nave Cornices as Elements of its Design and Structure," in Mark and Çakmak, eds., *Hagia Sophia from the Age of Justinian to the Present*, pp. 57ff. Though restored in subsequent centuries, the cornice belongs to the original edifice of the 530s and is composed of 215 blocks of Proconnesian marble which were assembled in a new way, different from earlier Constantinopolitan cornices, as Butler has shown.

53. In actuality the dome measures 30.85 m. along its east-west axis and 31.87 m. along the north-south axis.

54. According to the initial findings of a recent photogrammetric study of the dome: O. Gürkan, S. Camlidere, and M. Erdik, "Photogrammetric Studies of the Dome of Hagia Sophia," in Mark and Çakmak, eds., *Hagia Sophia from the Age of Justinian to the Present*, p. 82. Mainstone, *Hagia Sophia*, p. 65, gives the figure as 162 degrees.

55. The average width of these windows at the sill is approximately 1.60 m., while the forty window buttresses in the drum average 1.10 m. (according

to R. L. Van Nice's field notes, as quoted by Majeska, *Russian Travelers*, p. 233, nn. 179-180).

56. W. Emerson and R. L. Van Nice, "Hagia Sophia: The Collapse of the First Dome," *Archaeology* 4 (1951), p. 100.

57. Procopius, *De aed* I.i.44-45 (trans. Mango, *Art of the Byzantine Empire*, p. 75).

58. Procopius, *De aed* I.i.46; *Iliad*, VIII.19.

59. Procopius, *De aed* I.i.27 (trans. G. Downey, in Loeb Classical Library, pp. 12-13).

60. Procopius, *De aed* I.i. 47 (trans. Mango, *Art of the Byzantine Empire*, p. 75).

61. That the large columns are of verde antico is accepted by all scholars except A. M. Schneider, in *Byzantinische Zeitschrift* 37 (1937), p. 185, who identifies them as a green conglomerate from Thessaly in Greece.

62. The only exception known to me is a Hellenistic tomb facade of molded and painted plaster at Lefkadia (Leucadia) in Macedonia, dated to the late fourth or early third century B.C.: M. Robertson, *A Shorter History of Greek Art* (Cambridge, 1981), fig. 241. In the main facade of the stage building of the second century A.D. Roman theater at Aspendos, one finds a lack of congruence in the disposition of the niches (but not columns): K. Lanckoronski, ed., *Städte Pamphyliens und Pisidiens*, vol. 1 (Prague and Vienna, 1890-92), pls. XXIIf-XXIII. Early Byzantine church buildings sometimes displayed windows arranged in asymmetrical groupings--e.g., in the churches of the Acheiropoietos and St. Demetrius at Thessaloniki (fifth and sixth centuries, respectively).

63. The gallery colonnades of the Studius basilica are today destroyed. Column bases preserved above the nave entrances reveal that the narthex gallery opened onto the nave through a colonnade, just as did the galleries above the side aisles (Mathews, *Early Churches of Constantinople*, p. 23 and pl. 10). For an illustration of the elevation of SS. Sergius and Bacchus: T. F. Mathews, *The Byzantine Churches of Istanbul: A Photographic Survey* (University Park, 1976), fig. 29-15.

64. *Descr. S. Sophiae*, verses 392-394 (trans. Mango, *Art of the Byzantine Empire*, p. 81).

65. So Mainstone, *Hagia Sophia*, pp. 191ff.

66. The historical sources concerning the collapse of the first dome are collected and discussed by Mango, "Byzantine Writers," pp 51-53.

67. Agathias, *The Histories*, V.9.1-3 (trans. Mango, "Byzantine Writers," p. 52).

The inclination of the main piers from the vertical is 59.7 cm. (Mango, *Byzantine Architecture*, p. 64).

68. Sixth-century Byzantine writers report that the original dome was 6.20 to 7.7 m. lower than the second dome but do not specify the type of dome. Hence a number of scholars have endeavored to reconstruct the original dome. See, most recently, R. Taylor, "A Literary and Structural Analysis of the First Dome on Justinian's Hagia Sophia, Constantinople," *Journal of the Society of Architectural Historians,* 55 (1996), pp. 66ff., with earlier bibliography. Taylor proposes a "platter" dome about twenty feet shallower than the present dome and resting upon a fenestrated drum. For Taylor the principal documentary evidence for a fenestrated dome is Procopius's comparison of the original dome of the Justinianic St. Sophia and the fenestrated drum of the central dome of the Church of the Holy Apostles in Constantinople as rebuilt by Justinian and completed around 550 (and demolished in 1469). See Procopius, *De aed* I.4.14-16 (English translation in Taylor, p. 72). Cf. A. Çakmak, R. Taylor, and E. Durukal, "Hagia Sophia: A Possible Reconstruction of the First Dome," *Abstracts of Papers, Twenty-Second Annual Byzantine Studies Conference,* University of North Carolina at Chapel Hill (1996), p. 25.

69. Agathias, who saw both the first and second domes of the church, reports that the second dome "was narrower and steeper so that it did not strike spectators with as much amazement as before" (*The Histories,* V.9.3; trans. Mango, "Byzantine Writers," p. 52).

70. Martindale, *Prosopography of the Later Roman Empire,* vol. 3A, p. 724 ("Isidorvs 3").

71. Procopius, *De aed* II.11.8-9; *Inscriptiones grecques et latines de la Syrie,* ed. L. Jalabert, R. Mouterde et al, vol. 2 (Paris, 1959) nos. 348-349. See now J.-P. Fourdrin, "Une porte urbaine construite à Chalcis de Syrie par Isidore de Milet le Jeune (550/551)," *Travaux et Mémoires* 12 (1994), pp. 349ff.

72. Procopius, *De aed.* II.8.8-25. For John of Constantinople, Martindale, *Prosopography of the Later Roman Empire,* vol. IIIA, p. 662 ("Ioannes 49"). Cf. Fourdrin, *loc.cit.*

73. The Byzantine documents are assembled and assessed by Mango, "Byzantine Writers," pp. 54-55. For Trdat, see the Armenian historian Stephen of Tarōn II.13 and II.27 (ed. F. Macler, *Etienne Asolik de Tarōn* [Paris, 1917], and J. Strzygowski, *Die Baukunst der Armenier und Europa* (Vienna, 1918), I, pp. 590ff. For a detailed analysis of his repair work on the western arch and dome of St. Sophia, see Emerson and Van Nice, "Haghia Sophia, Istanbul," pp. 429ff.

74. Consult R. J. Mainstone, "The Reconstruction of the Tympana of St.

Sophia at Istanbul," *Dumbarton Oaks Papers* 23/24 (1969/1970), pp. 353ff.; *idem, Hagia Sophia*, pp. 97-98, 125. Describing the church shortly after its reconsecration in 562, Paul the Silentiary says that each tympanum as rebuilt in 562 featured "twice four windows" (*Descr. S. Sophiae*, vv. 534-537; trans. Mango,`Art of the Byzantine Empire*, pp. 83f.). Exactly how these eight windows were arranged is not indicated. Quite possibly there was a row of seven windows at the foot of each tympanum, and one large window above, of the same general type as the present great west window (Mainstone, *Hagia Sophia*, p. 125 and plans A5-A6).

75.   Mango, "Byzantine Writers," p. 54, for the document on these buttresses.

76.   Mainstone, *Hagia Sophia*, p. 104 and fig. 127. This is not to say that they were designed with the same structural properties as the flyers of Gothic cathedrals in western Europe. The pair of flying buttresses at the east end of the church are later, perhaps thirteenth-century Byzantine or Ottoman (*ibid.*, p. 104 and fig. 130).

77.   W. Emerson and R. L. Van Nice, "Hagia Sophia and the First Minaret Erected after the Conquest of Istanbul," *American Journal of Archaeology* 54 (1950), pp. 28ff.

78.   Mainstone, *Hagia Sophia*, p. 113.

79.   *Ibid.*, p. 114.

80.   For the restoration work of the Fossatis, see Gaspare Fossati, *Aya Sofia Constantinople, as Recently Restored by Order of H. M. The Sultan Abdul Medjid* (London, 1852), which consists of twenty-five colored lithographs showing exterior and interior views of the church both before and after the restoration. During their work on the building the Prussian architect Wilhelm Salzenberg spent five months in Constantinople and had access to St. Sophia, even ascending the scaffolds that had been erected. He published results of his findings, including measured plans and sections of the mosque, in the text and album of his *Alt-christliche Baudenkmale von Constantinopel vom V. bis XII. Jahrhundert* (Berlin, 1855). For a discussion of the Fossati's work on the church, see C. Mango, *Materials for the Study of the Mosaics of St. Sophia at Istanbul* (Washington, D.C., 1962), pp. 7ff.

81.   The placards were taken down when the mosque was secularized but were reinstalled in 1948.

82.   If a Pantokrator had been placed in the dome soon after the end of Iconoclasm, it would have been remade when the dome was repaired in the fourteenth century.

83.   *Ibid.*, pp. 15, 90-91.

84.   For a succinct account of these mosaics, with illustrations, see C. Mango

82   W. EUGENE KLEINBAUER

in H. Kähler and C. Mango, *Hagia Sophia* (New York, 1967), pp. 47ff. The dating and meaning of many of these mosaics are controversial in modern scholarship.

85. For the cross in mosaic in Justinian's second central dome, see *infra.*

86. *Descr. S. Sophiae,* v. 605 (trans. Mango, *Art of the Byzantine Empire,* p. 85).

87. *Ibid.*

88. Mathews, *Early Churches of Constantinople,* p. 91. An atrium strikingly close in design to that of the sixth-century St. Sophia has been established in the Justinianic church of St. John at Ephesus, completed by 565 (Krautheimer, *Early Christian and Byzantine Architecture,* 4th ed., fig. 196). No evidence intimates that the church and its courtyards were enclosed by an outer perimeter wall, as had existed at other sites--e.g., the cathedral at Tyre on the Lebanese coast, dedicated in ca. 315, according to Eusebius, *Ecclesiastical History* X.iv.37ff. (trans. J. E. L. Oulton, Loeb Classical Library [London , 1964], vol. 2, pp. 420ff.

89. *The Histories* V.6 (ed. Frendo, p. 137). However, for mention of an outer circuit wall in the year 1403, see Ruy González de Clavijo, *Embassy to Tamerlane 1403-1406,* tr. G. Le Strange (London, 1928), p. 76.

90. The sultan Selim II (1566-74) razed dwellings surrounding the mosque and replaced them with courtyards (Mathews, *Early Churches of Constantinople,* p. 100, n. 43).

91. G. J. Grelot, *Relation nouvelle d'un voyage de Constantinople* (Paris, 1680).

92. Paul the Silentiary, *Descr. S. Sophia,* verses 563-67. In the tenth-century "Book of Ceremonies" (*De ceremoniis* II, 22) of the emperor Constantine Porphyrogenetus it is referred to as the Great Baptistery. Just to the north of the center of the outer north perimeter wall of St. Sophia lies a hypogaeum: F. Dirimtekin, "Ayasofya imalindeki Vezir bahçesi denilen yerde bulunan bir hipogee," *Istanbul Arkeoloji Müzesi Y ll i* 10 (1962), pp. 30ff., pls. III-V; for its plan, Van Nice, *St. Sophia in Istanbul,* vol. 1, pl. 1 = my Fig. 2. This hypogaeum is dated to the beginning of the fifth century A.D.: Müller-Wiener, *Bildlexikon,* p. 84.

93. S. Eyice, "Le baptistère de Sainte Sophie d'Istanbul," *Atti del IX Congresso internationale di archeologia cristiana, Roma 21-27 settembre 1975.* Studi di antichità cristiana, 32 (Vatican City, 1978), vol. 2, pp. 257ff.; Mainstone, *Hagia Sophia,* p. 124 and figs. 140-141. S. Ristow, *Frühchristliche Baptisterien,* Jahrbuch für Antike und Christentum, Ergänzungsband 27 (Münster, 1998), pp. 246f., no. 668.

94. R. Cormack and E. J. W. Hawkins, "The Mosaics of St. Sophia at Istanbul: The Rooms above the Southwest Vestibule and Ramp," *Dumbarton Oaks*

Papers 31 (1977), pp. 175ff., identify these chambers as the large *sekreton* and the small *sekreton* of the Patriarchal Palace and attribute their construction to the emperor Justin II (565-78). For the Patriarchal Palace, see A. Pasadaios, *Ho Patriarchikos eikos tou Oikoumenikou Thronou* ["The patriarchal palace of the ecumenical throne"] (Thessaloniki, 1976), in modern Greek, with French resume (pp. 151-60).

95. F. Dirimtekin, "Le local du Patriarcat à Sainte Sophie," *Istanbuler Mitteilungen* 13/14 (1963/64), pp. 113ff.

96. See n. 43 *supra*. For the function of St. Sophia's *skeuophylakion*, see N. K. Moran, "The Skeuophyklakion of the Hagia Sophia," *Cahiers archéologiques* 34 (1986), pp. 29ff. In the 1970s a baptistery and a *skeuophylakion* were uncovered along the north flank of the Justinianic church of St. John at Ephesus: M. Büyükkolanci, "Zwei neu gefundene Bauten der Johannes-Kirche von Ephesos: Baptisterium und Skeuophylakion," *Istanbuler Mitteilungen* 32 (1982), pp. 236ff., who dates the baptistery to the fifth century and the treasury building to the end of the sixth or the beginning of the seventh century.

97. Mainstone, *Hagia Sophia*, p. 124. For the Constantinopolitan tradition of exterior stair ramps placed at the corners of church buildings, see Mathews, *Early Churches of Constantinople*, pp. 93f. and *passim*.

97a. Socrates, *H.E* II.16 (Migne, *P.G.* 67, col. 217); R. Janin, *La géographie écclesiastique de l'empire byzantin.* Ière partie: Le siège de Constantinople et le Patriarcat Oecumenique, vol. 3: *Les églises et les monastères*, 2d ed. (Paris, 1969), pp. 103f.

97b. Janin, *op.cit.*, pp. 237ff.; Mathews, *Early Churches of Constantinople*, pp. 28ff.; Müller-Wiener, *Bildlexikon*, pp. 76ff. (Acem Aga Mescidi)

97c. A novella of Justinian (535) describes the Great Church of Constantinople as consisting of St. Sophia, a church of Helena (otherwise unknown), the church of St. Theodore built by Sphorakios who was consul in 452, and a church of the Virgin built by the empress Verina: A. H. M. Jones, *The Late Roman Empire, 284-602*, vol. 1 (London, 1964), pp. 900f. and note 71 on p. 1375 for the Greek text of the novella; G. Dagron, *Naissance d'une capitale. Constantinople et ses institutions de 330 à 451* (Paris, 1974), p. 508, n.5; Janin, *op.cit.*, pp. 152f.

98. F. W. Deichmann, "Säule und Ordnung in der frühchristlichen Architektur," *Römische Mitteilungen*, 55 (1940), pp.114ff., reprinted in his *Rom, Ravenna, Konstantinopel, Naher Osten* (Wiesbaden, 1982), pp. 159ff., with an illustrated postscript on p. 186, analyzes the development of the classical orders in the period from the fourth to sixth centuries. See also note 61 *supra*. For revetments in late antiquity, see F. Rickert, "Inkrustation,"

Reallexikon für Antike und Christentum, facs. 138 (1997), cols. 160-179, esp. 174f.

99.   Especially J.-M. Spieser, *Thessalonique et ses monuments du IVe au VIe siècle* (Athens, 1984), pp. 165ff.

100. Procopius, *De aed* I.1.59-60 (trans. Mango, *Art of the Byzantine Empire*, p. 76).

101. *Descr. S. Sophiae* verse 605 (trans. Mango, *Art of the Byzantine Empire*, p. 85). This passage refers to either the walls of the atrium or the fountain in its midst.

102. *Descr. S. Sophiae.*, verse 617 (trans. Mango, *Art of the Byzantine Empire*, p. 85).

103. *Descr. S. Sophiae*, verses 617-46, 664-67 (trans. Mango, *Art of the Byzantine Empire*, pp. 85f.). Still useful is the description of all the surviving early Byzantine marbles in the church by Lethaby and Swainson, *Church of Sancta Sophia*, pp. 234ff.

104. For Proconnesian marble, see N. Asgari, "Roman and Early Byzantine Marble Quarries of Proconnesus," *Proceedings of the Xth International Congress of Classical Archaeology, Ankara-Izmir, 23-30/IX/ 1973,* ed. E. Akurgal (Ankara, 1973), vol. 1, pp. 467ff. The quarry in the Sea of Marmara is still being worked. For the green bands in the pavement, see G. Majeska, "Notes on the Archeology of St. Sophia at Constantinople: The Green Marble Bands in the Floor," *Dumbarton Oaks Papers* 32 (1978), pp.299ff. For the marble trade and workers in the early Byzantine period, see J.-P. Sodini, "Le commerce des marbres à l'époque protobyzantine," in *Hommes et richesses dans l'Empire byzantin*, vol. 1: *IVe-VIIe siècle* (Paris, 1989), pp. 163ff.

105. A. Kleinert, "Die Inkrustation der Hagia Sophia: Zur Entwicklung der Inkrustationsschemata im römischen Kaiserreich," Inaugural doctoral dissertation (Münster, 1979); summary in *Das Münster* 34 (1981), pp. 245f..

106. The original dome and vaults seem to have featured an aniconic gold ground (Procopius, *De aed* I.1.56; trans. Mango, *Art of the Byzantine Empire*, p. 76).

107. Paul the Silentiary, *Descr. S. Sophiae*, verses 489, 506 (trans. Mango, *Art of the Byzantine Empire*, p. 83).

108. For the carved capitals: R. *Kautzsch, Kapitellstudien; Beiträge zu einer Geschichte der spätantiken Kapitelle im Osten vom vierten bis ins siebente Jahrhundert* (Berlin, 1936), pp. 173f., 194ff., *passim;* F. W. Deichmann, *Studien zur Architektur Konstantinopels im 5. und 6. Jahrhundert n. Chr.* (Baden-Baden, 1956), pp. 76ff.; C. Strube, *Polyeuktos und Hagia Sophia. Umbildung und Auflösung antiker Formen. Entstehung des Kämpferkapitells* (Munich, 1984), pp. 93ff.; T. Zollt, *Kapitellplastik Konstantinopels vom 4. bis. 6. Jahrhundert n. Chr.; Mit einem Beitrag zur Untersuchung des ionischen Kämpferkapitells* (Bonn, 1994), pp. 254ff., *passim.*

109. Paul the Silentiary, *Descr. S. Sophiae*, verse 352 (trans. Mango, *Art of the Byzantine Empire*, p. 81), specifically states that the porphyry columns in the two eastern exedrae bore aloft golden capitals. See also pp.47f. *infra*.

110. *Ibid.*, verse 506 (trans. *ed.cit.*, p. 83).

111. Procopius, *De aed* I.i.30-31 (trans. Mango, *Art of the Byzantine Empire*, p. 74).

112. S. Vitale: C. Cecchelli, "Vetri di finestra del S. Vitale di Ravenna," *Felix Ravenna* n.s. 25, fasc. 2 (1930), pp. 1ff.. At Amorium fragments of window glass have been uncovered by the spade embedded in plaster window frames: C. S. Lightfoot, *Bulletin of British Byzantine Studies*, 22 (1996), p. 37. For Constantinople: A. H. S. Megaw, "Notes on Recent Work of the Byzantine Institute in Istanbul," *Dumbarton Oaks Papers* 17 (1963), pp. 333ff., for stained glass fragments found at the Zeyrek Camii and the Kariye Camii in Constantinople. Cf. M. Vickers, "A Painted Window in Saint Sophia at Istanbul," *Dumbarton Oaks Papers* 37 (1983), pp. 165f. The present stained glass windows in the apse of St. Sophia were inserted in the nineteenth century. No evidence suggests that mica panes were set into the window gratings of Justinian's St. Sophia, as they were in S. Sabina at Rome in 422-32. The sixth-century church of St. Polyeuktos at Constantinople was highly fenestrated, and pieces of colored window glass has been found at the site: R. M. Harrison, *Excavations at Saraçhane in Istanbul*, vol. 1 (Princeton, 1986), pp. 204ff.

113. Translation by L. Rodley, "Inauguration Anthem of Hagia Sophia in Edessa" (cited above in n. 13), p. 141.

114. *Ibid.*, p. 146. An analogous relationship of the concepts of light and wisdom is found in the Syriac inauguration anthem written for the new domed cathedral of St. Sophia at Edessa in Syria, built in the 540s or 550s (*ibid.*, pp. 147ff., with translation and commentary, and earlier bibliography).

115. *Descr. S. Sophiae*, verses 806ff. (trans. Mango, *Art of the Byzantine Empire*, pp.89ff.)

116. *Descr. S. Sophiae*, verse 884 (trans. Mango, *Art of the Byzantine Empire*, p. 91). A different assessment of marble revetment is given by Agathias when he describes the fate of the honorary consul and *curator divinae domus* Anatolius during the great Constantinopolitan earthquake of December 14, 557: "Anatolius was sleeping at the time in his customary bedchamber. The apartment was adorned with a variety of marble plaques attached to the wall, of the kind that are lavishly and ostentatiously displayed by those who are inordinately fond of such superfluous and unnecessary bric-à-brac. One of these plaques, which was fastened to the wall next to the bed, was shaken loose from its fittings and wrenched off by the

violence of the tremors. It came down with all its weight on his head, and smashed his skull. He had barely enough time to utter a deep and muffled groan of pain and then sank back on his bed. Death had overtaken him" (*The Histories* V.3.11, ed. Frendo, p. 138). For this unfortunate soul, see Martindale, *Prosopography of the Later Roman Empire*, vol. 3A, p. 72, *s.v.* Anatolius 7. Tersely mentioning the "various types of marbles" in St. Sophia, Agathias (*ibid.*, V.6.8) refers the reader to the poem of Paul the Silentiary.

117. *De aed* I.1.65.

118. *Descr. S. Sophiae* verses 682ff. (trans. Mango, *Art of the Byzantine Empire*, pp. 87ff.). A considerable body of scholarly literature has been devoted to a reconstruction of the sanctuary and its fittings. Fundamental are S. G. Xydis, "The Chancel Barrier, Solea and Ambo of Hagia Sophia," *Art Bulletin* 29 (1947), pp. 1ff.; Mathews, *Early Churches of Constantinople,* pp. 96ff.

119. *Descr. S. Sophiae*, verse 720 (trans. Mango, *Art of the Byzantine Empire*, p. 88).

120. *Descr. S. Sophiae*, verse 755 (trans. Mango, *Art of the Byzantine Empire*, pp. 88f.). Cf. Mathews, *Early Churches of Constantinople*, p. 166. A parallel to this altar covering is provided by three altar cloths (one of purple, a second of gold, a third with pearls) which Archbishop Maximian of Ravenna donated to churches at Ravenna toward the mid-sixth century (Agnellus, *Liber Pontificalis* XXVII, c. 80; trans. Mango, *Art of the Byzantine Empire*, pp. 106f.)

121. *Descr. S. Sophiae* verses 686-711. The architrave was wide enough for lamplighters. On the development of early Byzantine chancel screens at Constantinople, based on archaeological and liturgical sources, see U. Peschlow, "Zum Templon in Konstantinopel." *Armos. Timetikos tomos ston KathēgētēN. K. Moutsopoulo gia ta 25. Chrona pneumatikēs tou prosphoras sto panepist mio*, vol. 3 (Thessaloniki, 1991), pp. 1449ff.

122. *Descr. Ambonis*, verses 50ff. (trans. Mango, *Art of the Byzantine Empire*, pp. 91ff.).

123. *Ibid.*, verse 191 (trans. Mango, *Art of the Byzantine Empire*, p. 94).

124. *Ibid.*, verses 224, 240 (trans. Mango, *Art of the Byzantine Empire*, p. 95).

125. *Ibid.*, verse 580 (trans. Mango, *Art of the Byzantine Empire*, p. 85). On the location of the *metatorium*, see Mathews, *Early Churches of Constantinople*, pp. 133f.

126. *Descr. S. Sophiae*, verse 586 (trans. Mango, *Art of the Byzantine Empire*, p. 85). Cf. Procopius, *De aed* I.1.55-58. (trans. Mango, *loc.cit.*, p. 76). Mathews, *Early Churches of Constantinople*, pp. 128ff., 164, questions that women were assigned only to the galleries during the liturgy in the age of Justinian. The matter is beyond the scope of this study.

127. In the time of Justinian the text of the liturgy in St. Sophia was ascribed to John Chrysostom. Consult the engaging interpretation of it by G. Downey, *Constantinople in the Age of Justinian* (Norman, Ok., 1960), pp. 114ff.; and especially the instructive observations of R. Taft, "The Liturgy of the Great Church: An Initial Synthesis of Structure and Interpretation on the Eve of Iconoclasm," *Dumbarton Oaks Papers* 34/35 (1980/81), pp. 45ff. Because the essential elements of the liturgy performed in St. Sophia in the time of Justinian remain in doubt, it is reckless to attempt to derive the concept or design of the church from liturgical practice. For processions to and from St. Sophia, see J. F. Baldovin, *The Urban Character of Christian Worship: The Origins, Development and Meaning of Stational Liturgy*, Orientalia Christiana Analecta, 228 (Rome, 1987), pp. 181ff.

128. Mathews, *Early Churches of Constantinople*, p. 97.

129. Moorhead, *Justinian*, p. 52.

130. Ward-Perkins, "Structure and Building Methods" (cited in n. 42 supra), pp. 52ff., for a fundamental survey of buildings before and during the reign of Justinian (but oddly omitting SS. Sergius and Bacchus). For the materials of the present St. Sophia, see the two reports by Emerson and Van Nice: "Hagia Sophia, Istanbul: Preliminary Report," (cited in n,. 45 *supra*), pp. 403ff. and "Hagia Sophia: The Construction of the Second Dome and its Later Repairs," *Archaeology* 4 (1951), pp. 94ff., 162ff. Cf. Mainstone, *Hagia Sophia*, pp. 67ff.

131. *Ibid.*, p. 69.

132. Greenstone is a kind of disintegrated granite which presumably comes from the vicinity of Constantinople, but the exact location of the quarries is not known. Apparently occurring only in buildings of Justinian, it was used for the lower courses of structures for enhanced strength. See F. Dirimtekin, "Le Skevophylakion de Sainte-Sophie," *Revue des études byzantines*, 19 (1961), pp. 390ff.

133. Procopius, *De aed* I.i.53, mistakenly claims that lead was poured into the joints of the piers. This may be a *topos* suggested by Flavius Josephus, *De antiqua* XV.11.3. Sheets of lead have been discovered at the springing of the big arches: W. Emerson and R. Van Nice, "Hagia Sophia: The Collapse of the First Dome," *Archaeology*, 4 (1951), pp. 100., fig. 10. Paul the Silentiary, *Descr. S. Sophiae*, verses 476-80, correctly reports that "in the joints they have put sheets of soft lead lest the stones, pressing as they do upon one another and adding rude weight to weight, should have their backs broken; but with the lead inserted, the stone foundation is gently compressed (trans. Mango, *Art of the Byzantine Empire*, p. 83). Cf. Agathias,

The Histories, V.9.2 (trans. Frendo, p. 143), who claims that the church is built "of baken brick and lime on a structure of iron girders." Only a portion of the substructures of St. Sophia have been examined (see note 156 infra). For the report of a stonemason (*lithoxoos*) named Kalakalos in the tenth century or later who "while pouring lead into a hole of a building" near one of the two churches of St. Photeine at Constantinople "was accidentally blinded by splashing molten lead": A.-M. Talbot and A. Kazhdan, in *Byzantinische Forschungen* 20 (1994), p. 108.

134. For these bronze doors, see C. Bertelli, "Notizia preliminare sul restauro di alcune porte di S. Sofia a Istanbul," *Bollettino dell'Istituto Centrale de Restauro* 34/35 (1958), pp. 95ff. For the name 'imperial doors," see the tenth-century source of Constantine Porphyrogenitus, *De cerimoniis* 14-15 (ed. A. Vogt, *Le Livre des ceremonies*, vo. 1 [Paris, 1935] I.11).

135. Ward-Perkins, "Structure and Building Methods," pp. 71ff.; Mainstone, *Hagia Sophia*, pp. 69ff., passim.

136. *Ibid.*, pp. 69, 200, who reports that mineralogical examination of the large bricks has indicated that they were not manufactured from local clays. In an unpublished paper kindly sent to me by Professor A.S. Çakmak, which he co-authored with A. Moropoulou ("Provenance and Technology of the Hagia Sophia Ceramics"), the authors show that the clay used in the dome–but not the walls–of the structure came from Rhodes, and that the bricks themselves were manufactured locally in Constantinople.

137. Ward-Perkins, "Notes on the Structure and Building Methods," p. 72, n 1. R. Mark and A.S. Çakmak, "Mechanical Tests of Material from the Hagia Sophia Dome," *Dumbarton Oaks Papers* 48 (1994), pp. 277ff., provisionally report that the tensile strength of the Byzantine mortar in the sixth-century dome is two to three times the strength of specimens of medieval lime mortar. See also A.S. Çakmak et al, "Interdisciplinary Study of Dynamic Behavior and Earthquake Response of Hagia Sophia," in *Soil Dynamics and Earthquake Engineering*, 14 (1995), pp. 125-33.

138. Procopius, *De aed* I.iv.1-8. See Mathews, *Early Churches of Constantinople*, pp. 42ff.

139. Agathias, *The Histories* V.9.2 (ed. Frendo, p. 143).

140. Mathews, *Early Churches of Constantinople*, pp. 42ff.; Müller-Wiener, *Bildlexikon*, pp. 177ff.; P. Grossmann, "Beobachtungen zum ursprünglichen Grundriss der Sergios- und Bakchoskirche in Konstantinopel," *Istanbuler Mitteilung* 39 (1989), pp. 153ff.; I. Shadîd, "The Church of Sts. Sergius and Bacchus in Constantinople: Who Built It and Why?" *Abstracts of Papers, Twenty-Second Annual Byzantine Studies Conference*, University of North Carolina at Chapel Hill (1996), p. 84.

141. Mainstone, *Hagia Sophia*, p. 157. Only the lowest third of the dome has been investigated: P. Sanpaolesi, "La chiesa dei ss. Sergio e Bacco a Costantinopoli," *Rivista dell'Istituto nazionale d'archeologia e storia dell'arte*, n.s. 10 (1961), pp. 116ff., who reported that this section is constructed of slightly pitched bricks. The upper parts of the dome, not seen by him, may well be made of some lighter material, but this needs to be confirmed.

142. See n. 10 *supra*.

143. For the Greek inscription, see Henderson, "SS. Sergius and Bacchus, Constantinople" (cited in n. 10 *supra*), p. 7 and fig. 5; See also H. Swainson, "Monograms on the Capitals of S. Sergius at Constantinople," *Byzantinische Zeitschrift* 4 (1895), pp. 106ff.

144. So C. Mango, "The Church of Saints Sergius and Bacchus at Constantinople and the Alleged Tradition of Octagonal Palatine Chapels," *Jahrbuch der Österreichischen Byzantinistik* 2 (1972), pp. 189ff., with a critical analysis of the textual sources bearing on the problem of dating.

145. Cited by Mathews, *Early Churches of Constantinople*, p. 47 and n. 26.

146. For the upper cornice of St. Sophia, Mainstone, *Hagia Sophia*, pp. 61ff.; and n. 52 *supra*.

147. Translated in W. R. Paton, *The Greek Anthology*, Loeb Classical Library (Cambridge, Mass., 1960), I, pp. 6-11.

148. C. Mango and I. Ševčenko, "Remains of the Church of St. Polyeuktos at Constantinople," *Dumbarton Oaks Papers* 15 (1961), pp. 243ff.

149. R. M. Harrison, *Excavations at Saraçhane in Istanbul*, vol. 1 (Princeton, 1986). J. W. Hayes published the pottery as volume 2 (Princeton, 1992). A more popular volume of the church which contains numerous color illustrations was also issued by Harrison: *A Temple for Byzantium: The Discovery and Excavation of Anicia Juliana's Palace-Church in Istanbul* (London, 1989).

150. J. Bardill, "Brickstamps and the Date of St. Polyeuktos," *Bulletin of British Byzantine Studies* 20 (1994), p. 67. The possibility of the earlier dating is entertained by G. Fowden, "Constantine, Silvester and the Church of S. Polyeuctus in Constantinople," *Journal of Roman Archaeology* 7 (1994), pp. 274f. The evidence offered by the brickstamps is suggestive but inconclusive. Harrison, *Excavations at Saraçhane*, pp. 111f., believes all the archaeological evidence favors a dating of 524 to 527.

151. So Harrison, *Excavations at Saraçhane*, I, p. 420. Cf. C. Milner, "The Image of the Rightful Ruler: Anicia Juliana's Constantine Mosaic in the Church of Hagios Polyeuktos," in *New Constantines: The Rhythm of Imperial Renewal*

90 W. EUGENE KLEINBAUER

   in Byzantium, 4th-13th Centuries, ed. P. Magdalino (Aldershot, 1994), pp. 73ff. Fowden, *loc.cit.*, sees a clear religious as well as political statement made by the patron in building her church.

152. Harrison, *Excavations at Saraçhane*, I. p. 420.

153. *Anth. Pal.* I.10.47-49. See R. M. Harrison, "The Church of St. Polyeuktos in Istanbul and the Temple of Solomon," *Okeanos = Harvard Ukrainian Studies*, 7 (1983), pp. 276ff.; idem, *Temple for Byzantium*, pp. 137ff.

154. *Ibid.*, p. 132.

155. Harrison, *Excavations at Saraçhane*, p. 410.

156. Emerson and Van Nice, "Hagia Sophia, Istanbul" (cited in n. 45 *supra*), pp. 407ff. and fig. 3, report on their explorations of more than 300 m. of passages underlying the western part of the nave and the two narthexes of St. Sophia.

157. As, for example, in the case of the Bodrum Camii at Constantinople, built before 922: Müller-Wiener, *Bildlexikon*, pp. 103ff., and figs. 82, 84; C. L. Striker, *The Myrelaion (Bodrum Camii) in Istanbul* (Princeton, 1981).

158. As suggested by J. C. Smith, in *Journal of the Society of Architectural Historians 51* (1992), p. 217.

159. Krautheimer, *Early Christian and Byzantine Architecture*, 4th ed. rev., pp. 219, 245.

160. *Ibid.*, pp. 249ff., with the older bibliography cited in note 23 on p. 489. This possibility is also raised by Harrison, *Excavations at Saraçhane*, p. 407. The exact form of the Justinianic design of Hagia Eirene cannot be firmly ascertained because of the rebuilding of the church in the eighth century.

161. Hill, *Early Byzantine Churches* (see n. 46 *supra*), pp. 46ff. and *passim*.

162. *Ibid.*, p. 54; M. Gough, "The Emperor Zeno and some Cilician Churches," *Anatolian Studies* 22 (1972), pp. 199ff.

163. Harrison, *Excavations at Saraçhane*, p. 407; Hill, *Early Byzantine Churches*, pp. 226ff., fig. 44, pl. 99, with earlier bibliography.

164. Exploring the church remains in 1907 with Ernst Herzfeld, Samuel Guyer became convinced that a massive masonry dome covered the east bay of the nave (in E. Herzfeld and S. Guyer, *Meriamlik und Korykos. Zwei christliche Ruinenstätten des Rauhen Kilikiens* (Manchester, 1930), pp. 61f. Later examining the remains G. H. Forsyth argued in favor of a wooden pyramid over the east bay and an ordinary wood roof over the west bay: "Architectural Notes on a Journey through Cilicia," *Dumbarton Oaks Papers* 11 (1957), pp. 223ff., esp. 224-225. Part of his argument depended on his interpretation of the known superstructure of the East Church at

Alahan Manastir (see *infra*). Forsyth's observations and conclusions are accepted by H. Hellenkemper, "Die Kirchenstiftung des Kaisers Zenon im Wallfahrtsheiligtum der heiligen Thekla bei Seleukia," *Wallraf-Richartz-Jahrbuch* 47 (1986), pp. 63ff. Recently, Hill, *Early Byzantine Churches*, shows why the comparison of Meryemlik and Alahan Manastir is not as direct as Forsyth and Hellenkemper would have it, and, more importantly, why a central nucleus covered by a dome in masonry remains a strong possibility.

165. For a description of this church, see G. Bakker, "The Buildings at Alahan," in M. Gough, ed., *Alahan: an Early Christian Monastery in Southern Turkey Based on the Work of Michael Gough* (Toronto, 1985), pp. 102-19. For the identification of Alahan as a center of pilgrimage, see Hill, *Early Byzantine Churches*, p. 8; C. Mango, in *Jahrbuch der Österreichischen Byzantinistik*, 41 (1991), pp. 298-300.

166. Arguments supporting a dome are presented by Hill, *Early Byzantine Churches*, pp. 78ff., who believes that the east bay was roofed over by a wood dome.

167. *Ibid.*, pp.155ff., pls 64-70, and fig. 28, with earlier bibliography. Hill dates this church to the reign of Justinian, but this cannot be substantiated.

168. This reconstruction is offered by Hill, *op.cit.*, pp. 46, 155ff., who objects to the suggestion of a wood pyramid over the nucleus of the church that had earlier been proposed by Forsyth, *op.cit.*, p. 235. Forsyth's proposal had been accepted by M. Gough who excavated the church ruin in 1958: "The Emperor Zeno," pp. 199ff., esp. 203ff. For two other churches in Isauria and Cilicia that may have been domed-- one at Alakilise and the Tomb Church at Corycus, see Hill, *Early Byzantine Churches,* pp. 45ff., *passim*.

169. *Ibid.*, p. 47, an "audience chamber" or Christian (?) mausoleum rather than a church. For this monument consult R. W. Edwards, "The Domed Mausoleum at Akkale in Cilicia: The Byzantine Revival of a Pagan Plan," *Byzantinoslavica* 50 (1989), pp. 46ff. (here dated between the 480s and 520s). Fully developed spherical triangular pendentives are also recorded in the fifth century at Abu Mina in Egypt (P. Grossmann, *Abū Mīnā I. Die Gruftkirche und die Gruft* [Mainz, 1989], vol. 1, p. 232, pls. 49, a-c)) and in churches at Karabel and Alacahisar in Lycia attributed (correctly?) to early in the reign of Justinian: R. M. Harrison, "Churches and Chapels in Early Byzantine Lycia," *Anatolian Studies* 13 (1963), pp. 131-36, 148-50, respectively.

170. Hill, *Early Byzantine Churches*, p. 59, identifies the "Cupola Church" at Meryemlık as the prototype of the church of St. Polyeuktos at Constantinople.

171. C. Mango, "Isaurian Builders," *Polychronion. Festschrift Franz Dölger zum 75. Geburtstag*, ed. P. Wirth (Heidelberg, 1966), pp. 358ff.

172. See W. Eugene Kleinbauer, "The Aisled Tetraconch," Ph.D. dissertation, Princeton University, 1967; *idem*, "The Origin and Functions of the Aisled Tetraconch Churches in Syria and Northern Mesopotamia" *Dumbarton Oaks Papers* 27 (1973), pp. 89ff.; *idem*, "The Double-shell Tetraconch Building at Perge in Pamphylia and the Origin of the Architectural Genus," *op.cit.*, 41 (1987), pp. 277ff.

173. See, most recently, G. A. Dell'Acqua, ed., *La Basilica di San Lorenzo in Milano* (Milan, 1985), with earlier bibliography; "La basilica di S. Lorenzo," in *Milano: capitale dell'impero romano, 286-402 d.c.* (Milan, 1990), pp. 137ff..

174. "*Aedita in* turribus': The Superstructure of the Early Christian Church of S. Lorenzo at Milan," *Gesta*, 15 (1976), pp. 1ff. My reconstruction is accepted by Mainstone, *Hagia Sophia*, p. 149.

175. Kleinbauer, "Double-shell Tetraconch Building at Perge," pp. 277ff.

176. Kleinbauer, "Origin and Functions," pp. 89ff. In the eastern quarter of Bosra in Syria recent excavations have been uncovering part of the remains of a large central-plan edifice (termed by the excavator the "New Cathedral") which bears a striking resemblance to the aisled tetraconch church of SS. Sergius, Bacchus, and Leontius of 512/13 in the city, but this building, attributed to the end of the fifth or beginning of the sixth century, featured an interior circular ring of single columns inscribed in a square envelope rather than a quatrefoil disposition of elements: J.-M. Dentzer *et al*, "Nouvelles recherches franco-syriennes dans le quartier est de Bosra ash-Sham," *Comptes rendus, Académie des Inscriptions & Belles-Lettres*, January-March, 1993, pp. 117ff., figs. 1, 6; *idem*, in *Corso di cultura sull'arte ravennate e bizantina* (1988), pp. 13ff.; C. Foss, "Syria in Transition, A.D. 550-750: An Archaeological Approach," *Dumbarton Oaks Papers*, 51 (1997), pp. 240f., fig. 27.

176a. The most recent assessment of this building is Foss, *op.cit.*, pp. 215ff., figs. 17-18.

177. Choisy, *L'art de bâtir chez les Byzantins* (Paris, 1883), p. 131, fig. 136; *idem*, *Histoire de l'architecture (Paris, 1899)*, vol. 2, p. 41 fig. The photograph was first published by B. Filov, in *Godi nik na Narodnija archeologiceska muzei v Sofiia (= Annuaire du Musée national archéologique, Sofia)*, vol. 4 (1926), pp. 380f., fig. 127. The inconsistencies in Choisy's two plans are analyzed by Kleinbauer, *The Aisled Tetraconch*, and P. Grossmann, "Die zweischaligen spätantiken Vierkonchenbauten in Ägypten und ihre Beziehung zu den gleichartigen Bauten in Europa und Kleinasien," in *Das römisch-*

byzantinische Ägypten. Akten des internationalen Symposions 26.-30. September 1978 in Trier, ed. G. Grimm *et al* (Mainz, 1983), pp. 167ff., with a revised plan.

178. The Byzantine foot used for the church is approximately 0.312 m. (1.024 English feet), according to the calculations of Mainstone, *Hagia Sophia,* pp. 6, 177. See E. Schilbach, *Byzantinische metrologische Quellen* (Thessaloniki, 1982), on the variability of Byzantine measures. Cf. P. Underwood, "Some Principles of Measure in the Architecture of the Period of Justinian," *Cahiers archéologiques* 3 (1948), pp. 64ff.

179. Procopius, *De aed* I.i.67ff.

180. *Ibid., De aed* I.i.68-72.

181. *Ibid.,* I.i.74.

182. For these deformations, see Mainstone, *Hagia Sophia,* pp. 87ff., *passim.*

183. The 2.55 m. measurement is a calculation of R. L. Van Nice, "The Structure of St. Sophia," *Architectural Forum* (May, 1963), p. 138.

184. For a useful recent survey of late antique and Byzantine domes, see M. Restle, "Kuppel," *Reallexikon zur byzantinischen Kunst* 5 (1995), cols. 484ff. According to Restle, *Studien zur frühbyzantinischen Architektur Kappadokiens* (Vienna, 1979), pp. 146ff., stone domes can be first documented in Cappadocia in the mid-sixth century.

185. W. L. MacDonald, *The Pantheon* (London, 1976).

186. M. G. Salvadori, *Why Buildings Stand Up* (New York, 1980), pp. 242ff.

187. Choisy, *L'art de bâtir,* Mainstone, "Structure of the Church of St. Sophia," pp. 23ff.

188. The first published partial finite-element analysis is R. Mark and A. Westagard, "The First Dome of Hagia Sophia: Myth vs. Technology," in *Domes from Antiquity to the Present,* pp. 163ff., reprinted without significant change in R. Mark, *Light, Wind, and Structure: The Mystery of the Master Builders* (Cambridge, Mass., 1990), pp. 59ff., fig. 3.12. For the current modeling project at Princeton, consult R. Mark et al, "Preliminary Report on an Integrated Study of the Structure of Hagia Sophia: Past, Present, and Future," in Mark and Çakmak, eds., *Hagia Sophia from the Age of Justinian to the Present,* pp. 120ff.

189. The decagonal rotunda known as the Temple of Minerva Medica in Rome (diameter 25 m.) was covered by a concrete dome about a framework of brick ribs. Brick stamps date this edifice to 310 to 320. The slightly later concrete dome of Santa Costanza in Rome measures only about 7 m. in diameter.

190. In Constantinople the pre-Justinianic rotunda adjacent to the tenth-century church of the Myrelaion was intended to be capped by a dome 29.6 m. in diameter, but it is not known whether it was ever constructed: Müller-Wiener, *Bildlexikon*, pp. 240-44, fig. 85.

191. Boëthius and Ward-Perkins, *Etruscan and Roman Architecture* (Harmondsworth, 1970), pp 388f.; Ward-Perkins, "Structure and Building Methods," pp. 89, 100, pl. 27C.

192. *Ibid.*, p. 88.

193. A. M. Mansel, *Die Ruinen von Side* (Berlin, 1963), pp. 187ff., figs. 153-56; B. Brenk, *Spätantike und Frühes Christentum*, Propylaen Kunstgeschichte, Supplemental vol. 1 (Frankfurt, 1977), p. 165 and pl. 126.

194. As stated by M. Restle, "Kuppel," col. 506. At Thessaloniki Hosios David, possibly once a funerary or martyrial chapel attached to a larger (and destroyed) church, pendentive domes covered the four corner chambers, barrel vaults the cross arms, and presumably a larger, hemispherical dome on pendentives (the pendentives survive) over the center space--all constructed of brick and mortar: P. Grossmann, "Zur typologischen Stellung der Kirche von Hosios David in Thessalonike," *Felix Ravenna*, ser. 4 (1984-85), pp. 25ff. Although sometimes dated as early as the mid-fifth century on no good grounds, but more commonly ca. 500 A.D. (cf. Krautheimer, *Early Christian and Byzantine Architecture*, 4th ed., pp. 239ff.), this edifice may in fact be Justinianic; see Spieser, *Thessalonique*, pp 157f.

195. G. Penelis *et al*, "The Rotunda of Thessaloniki: Seismic Behavior of Roman and Byzantine Structures," in Mark and Çakmak, eds., *Hagia Sophia from the Age of Justinian*, p. 132, gives the dome's diameter as 24.5 m., Ward-Perkins (in n. 191 *supra*) as 24.15 m.

196. The Rotunda awaits a definitive final publication. H. Torp has promised a monograph based on a thorough examination of the structure launched by E. Dyggve in the late 1930s. A team of Greek specialists has been studying and restoring the structure and the mosaics in its dome since an earthquake struck Thessaloniki in 1978, but whether and when the Greeks will issue a final publication remain to be seen. See, however, the important preliminary report by K. Theocharidou, "The Rotunda at Thessaloniki. New Discoveries and Definitions after the Restoration works" (in modern Greek, with English summary), *Deltionētēs Christianikes Archaiologikes Hetaireias*, 4th series, vol. 16 (1991-92), pp. 57ff., esp. fig. 11 (for a detailed drawing of the masonries in the dome). Her report does not deal with the problem of the date of conversion of the Rotunda into a church, a matter of considerable controversy. On the

structure of the dome see also Penelis et al, "The Rotunda of Thessaloniki," pp. 132ff. Examination of the mosaics in 1952-53 by Dyggve and his assistant H. Torp persuasively demonstrated on archaeological grounds that the mosaics were executed when the masonry of the upper section of the dome was finished: H. Torp, "Quelques remarques sur les mosaïques de l'église de Saint-Georges à Thessaloniques," *Acts of the Ninth International Byzantine Congress, Thessaloniki, August 12-19, 1953* (title in modern Greek), vol. 1 (Athens, 1955), pp. 489ff. Cf. *idem, Mosaikkene I St Georg-Rotunden I Thessaloniki* (Oslo, 1963). Cf. W. Eugene Kleinbauer, "The Iconography and Date of the Mosaics of the Rotunda of Hagios Georgios, Thessaloniki," *Viator* 3 (1972), pp. 27ff., esp. 68ff., with a dating of the late 440s to the 470s.

197. As observed by Ward-Perkins, in Boëthius and Ward-Perkins, *Etruscan and Roman Architecture,* p. 524.

198. See n. 58 supra.

199. *Oration* XVIII.39 (trans. Mango, *Art of the Byzantine Empire,* p. 26 and n. 27, interpreting the text as referring to a dome ringed with many windows.

200. Procopius, *De aed* I.i.61-64.

201. Marcellinus *comes, Chron.* S.a. 537.5, ed. *The Chronicle of Marcellinus,* trans. and commentary by B. Croke (Sydney, 1995), p. 47. The following two items came to my attention too late to be incorporated into my manuscript: *Die Hagia Sophia in Istanbul.* Akten des Berner Kolloquiums vom 21. Oktober 1994. Ed. V. Hoffmann. Neue Berner Schriften zur Kunst, vol. 3 (Bern, 1997); C. Mango, *Hagia Sophia: A Vision for Empires* (Istanbul, 1998).

THE FREDERIC LINDLEY MORGAN CHAIR OF ARCHITECTURAL DESIGN is an endowed professorship which brings distinguished historians and designers to the Allen R. Hite Art Institute at the University of Louisville

MORGAN PROFESSORS

Alan Gowans, *University of Victoria*	1975
Lois Langhorst, *University of North Carolina*	1981
John Coolidge, *Harvard University*	1981
Colin McWilliam, *Heriot-Watt University*	1982
Clay Lancaster, *Salvisa, Kentucky*	1983
Sidney D. Markman, *Duke University*	1984
Leonard K. Eaton, *University of Michigan*	1985
Christopher Tadgell, *Canterbury College of Art*	1985
Pieter Singelenberg, *University of Utrecht*	1986
John James, *Sydney University*	1987
Labelle Prussin, *City University of New York*	1988
Osmund Overby, *University of Missouri*	1989
Thomas J. McCormick, *Wheaton College*	1991
Peter Willis, *University of Newcastle*	1992
Richard Betts, *University of Illinois*	1994
Eugene Kleinbauer, *Indiana University*	1995
Åsa Ringbom, *Åbo Akademi*	1996
Elizabeth C. Stone, *State University of New York at Stony Brook*	1997

Designed by William L. Bauhan and Sarah F. Bauhan.
Typeset in Janson Linotron by Sarah F. Bauhan.
Printed and bound by Thomson-Shore Inc., Dexter, Michigan.